Unto Us a Child

Abuse and Deception
in the Catholic Church

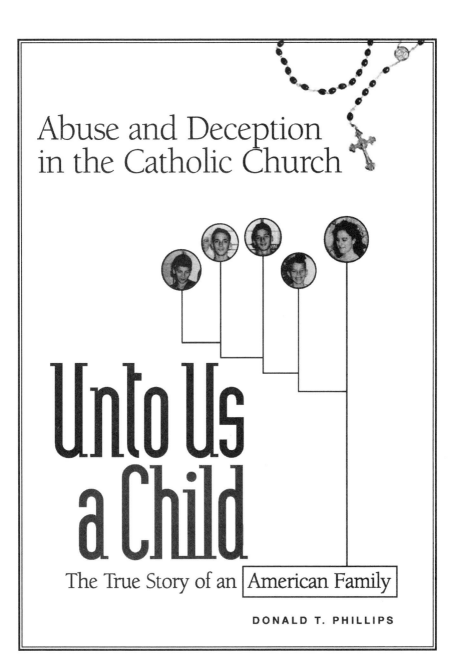

Unto Us
a Child

The True Story of an American Family

DONALD T. PHILLIPS

Tapestry Press
Irving, Texas

Tapestry Press
3649 Conflans Road
Suite 103
Irving, TX 75061
972 399-8856
info@tapestrypressinc.com
www.tapestrypressinc.com

Printed in the U.S.A.
06 05 04 03 02   1 2 3 4 5

Library of Congress Cataloging-in-Publication Data
 Phillips, Donald T. (Donald Thomas), 1952-
  Unto us a child : abuse and deception in the Catholic Church /
by Donald T. Phillips.
    p. cm.
  ISBN 1-930819-22-6 (hardcover : alk. paper)
   1. Catholic Church—United States—Clergy—Sexual behavior.
 2. Child sexual abuse by clergy—United States. 3. Adult child sex
ual abuse victims—United States—Biography. I. Title.
  BX1912.9 .P49 2002
  362.76'0973—dc21
                                        2002010952

Notice: Despite our best efforts, we were not able to identify the source of the
poem "Having a Husband" prior to printing. This poem can be found on the back
of Darlene's handmade birth announcement in the photographic section of *Unto
Us a Child*. It was presumably written by Helen Harrington, a twentieth-century
poet and author from Iowa. We have been unable to contact Ms. Harrington or
her heirs or to locate a published copy of the poem. We welcome any information
that our readers might have. Jill Bertolet, Publisher

Cover by David Sims

Book design and layout by
D. & F. Scott Publishing, Inc.
N. Richland Hills, Texas

"For unto us a child is born, unto us a son is given: and the government shall be upon his shoulder . . ."

Isaiah 9:6

Preface

This is a heartbreaking story. So heartbreaking, I almost couldn't write about it.

A friend of mine approached me one day and said he had a story that needed to be told. "Would you consider writing it?" he asked.

"Well, maybe," I said. "I'm in the middle of a book right now. But, tell me about it."

"My father had eight sisters and brothers," he began. "Two of them died very young. All the rest were taken away from their parents and put in a Catholic orphanage in Kansas. Three of his four brothers were sexually and physically abused. The fourth won't talk about it. He also had two sisters. One we don't know too much about. The other had a baby by a priest. When they found out she was pregnant, they sent her off to a Catholic-run home for unwed mothers. She was admitted under an assumed name, had her baby, and then was sent back. The baby was put up for adoption."

"That's awful," I said quietly. I was also thinking that all this must have happened so long ago that it would be difficult to pull enough information together to tell the story accurately.

"Wait, that's not all," he continued. "My father was seduced by a nun when he was twelve years old. When he told me about it the other night he became so emotional he could barely talk about it. And it happened over forty years ago! It's that way with all of my uncles. They're tormented."

"What about your two aunts, the sisters?" I asked.

"They're dead. Both had mental problems. Both were alcoholics. One died in a halfway house, the other of a heart attack. When my Aunt Darlene died, she left behind a secret photo album. None of my uncles had ever seen it before. But it showed her "Catholic" family—the priest she was in love with, the orphanage, childhood photographs, things like that."

This was such a sad, hardly believable story, that I started tentatively, slowly. First I met with my friend's father—and then his uncles. The interviews were more like therapy sessions than anything else. But it quickly became clear that they were all telling the truth and more than obvious that they were still emotionally affected. So I went to Wichita, visited all the sites, met and interviewed key people. With the brothers' help, I was able to track down other kids who were in the orphanage (now adults and living in various parts of the country). In addition, there turned out to be more than enough documents and witnesses to pull the entire tale together.

Initially, the Albert brothers did the right thing. They tried to get help from the Catholic Church. They went to local Church officials and explained what had happened. But they were not believed. Worse yet, they were accused of lying. Then the brothers took their story to court. But, overwhelmed by a powerful and wealthy organization, they were defeated—but not broken.

During the course of my work, I found the Alberts to be kind, decent, and amazingly resilient people. What happened to their family was unspeakable. How they were treated was wrong. They deserved better.

Well, the Catholic Diocese of Wichita wouldn't help them, but I will. Half of all author royalties are assigned to the Albert brothers.

Yes, this is a heartbreaking story. But it's a true story. And one that definitely needed to be told.

Donald T. Phillips
August 2002

Chapter One

A cold front had blown through Wichita overnight and snapped the temperatures down into the low teens. So when Ray Albert awoke early that morning the first thing he did was hustle into the kitchen to put on a pot of hot coffee. When his bare feet hit the kitchen tile, it sent a shiver through the rest of his body.

"Jesus, Mary, and Joseph!" he grumbled. "That's cold—even for January."

But at least it was Sunday, his day off. The only day of the week he got to rest. The other six days he was busy traveling around the state of Kansas setting up convenience stores. It was a pretty decent job, though. A bit lonely. But the money was good. The best thing about it was that it kept him busy. And at age fifty-four, Ray liked to keep busy.

After taking a hot shower and throwing on some warm clothes, Ray poured himself a cup of coffee and grabbed a stale doughnut. As he sat at the kitchen table and gazed out the window, he thought about it being Sunday and about all the people who must be getting ready to go to church.

"Church," he muttered. "Had enough of that long ago."

Then Ray's eyes wandered across his new one-bedroom apartment and he thought about all the unpacked boxes stacked in the closets. "This probably would be a good day to get some of those boxes cleaned out," he said to himself. "Yeah, better get after it."

So he wolfed down the rest of his doughnut, picked up his coffee mug, and walked over to the big closet in the living room. This particular space used to hold a fold-down Murphy bed. But somewhere along the way, one of the landlords had it removed.

Now, with its large double doors and long, narrow area, it was really good for nothing more than a storage area.

After drawing the doors back, Ray pulled out three of ten stacked apple boxes and sat down on the floor to go through them. He removed the top on the first box and was surprised to find a couple strands of lights, some tree ornaments, and a nativity setting.

"Christmas decorations," he said. "Oh, these must be Darlene's. I forgot all about this stuff."

After Ray's sister, Darlene, died five years before, he and his brothers and sister had gone into her apartment, boxed up all her belongings, and put them in storage. Eventually, they sold off the furniture and gave her clothes to charity, but several of the cartons had been placed in one of Ray's closets and had simply moved with him from apartment to apartment. With this latest move, boxes buried in the back of previous closets were now stacked on top. As a matter of fact, it was amazing that he still had any of this stuff at all, because, had he noticed it before, he would have thrown everything out.

Now, though, he would take the time to sift through his sister's personal effects. Besides, for a reason that he could not explain, Darlene had been on his mind recently. It made him sad to think that she was only forty-five years old when she died. Attractive, bright, and unusually reclusive, Darlene was meticulous by nature and a bit of a pack rat. She'd also dressed in black over the last twenty years of her life, and Ray had always wondered why.

The second box contained mostly odds and ends. There were lots of knickknacks, including several stuffed animals—a teddy bear, a rabbit, several small giraffes. There were four or five containers that had once held liquor—a replica of the Eiffel Tower, the leaning Tower of Pisa, an antique auto. Each was marked with a date and a place that noted when and where they were acquired. Darlene did the same for nearly everything in the boxes.

Then Ray pulled out a seventeen-year-old unopened bottle of bourbon and an untapped bottle of champagne. "Would you look at that," he whispered as he held a bottle in each of his hands. "Wonder what she was saving these for?"

Next, Ray reached in and carefully removed Darlene's statuettes of the Virgin Mary. His sister had collected them, loved them, kept them all around her apartment. There were six figurines in this particular box—four holding baby Jesus, two standing with arms opened. One was carved out of ivory and, as the label noted, stood on a "Genuine Carrara Marble" base and was "Made in Italy." Another had "Boys Town" imprinted on the back. Ray recalled it as the one his four younger brothers had given Darlene when she visited them up at the famous Father Flanagan home for boys in Nebraska. She had always cherished this particular figurine, he remembered.

The third box was filled with paperwork, including several folders of bank records, canceled checks, income tax statements, apartment lease agreements. There was a folder marked with the name Thomas J. Groetken, which Ray recognized as Darlene's husband. Inside were Tom's birth certificate, his honorable discharge from the Army after World War II, and an award for twenty-three years of service to the US Postal Service. Tom was twenty-seven years older than Darlene and had died of cancer in 1982 at age sixty-eight—so Ray wasn't surprised to find funeral paperwork along with his sister's applications for insurance and death benefits.

Ray next removed five high school yearbooks from the box. There were two from Walnut, Kansas, where she had been a freshman in 1958 at both a Catholic and public high school; one from her sophomore year, 1959, at El Dorado High School; and one each from her junior and senior years ('60 and '61) at Wichita North High School.

Beneath the annuals, Ray found a single manila folder lying flat on top of an old photo album. Inside was a round-trip bus ticket from Wichita to Kansas City, paper clipped to a dozen or so letters that were addressed to Darlene from the Missouri Department of Health and the Catholic Charities of Kansas City.

Quickly, Ray flipped through the letters and skimmed some of the paragraphs:

(May 1, 1985) Upon receipt of your request for a copy of your son's birth record, we made a search of the files and were unable to locate . . .

(February 25, 1986) We are trying to comply with your request for identifying information regarding your adoption. However . . .

(December 15, 1986) Attached is correspondence and case material from an adoption which occurred in Jackson County. The relinquishing parent wishes to contact her son . . .

(March 13, 1987) We had searched our court adoption files and nothing was found concerning the adoption of William Patrick Albert . . . I am sorry we could not be of more assistance to you.

"My God," thought Ray, who had never seen any of these letters, "this last one is dated just a few months before Darlene died. What in hell is going on here?"

Then Ray reached into the bottom of the box and pulled out the photo album—something else his sister had never shared with him. It had a cream white cover with pages of black construction paper (about thirty in all) filled on both sides with all manner of photographs. Each page was removable and bound together through two punch holes with a brown string. Actually, the whole thing appeared to be as much a scrapbook as a photo album.

Ray opened it up and found, centered on the first page, a five-by-seven-inch, black-and-white class photograph of kids from the St. Joseph Home for Children in El Dorado—where he and all his brothers and sisters had been placed back in 1950. Such photos were taken once a year, and Ray remembered posing for several during his time there. But he had already been gone from the place several years when this particular picture was taken. From the apparent ages of Darlene and his brothers, he figured that it must have been shot in 1957, just before she went into a foster home and the boys were sent to Boys Town. Also in the picture were nine other children and, as the orphanage was Catholic-run, four nuns and a priest.

At the top of the page, immediately above the five-by-seven, were three wallet-size photos. The one on the left was a young priest. On the right was Darlene. And in the middle was a picture of a little boy sitting with his legs crossed. But the boy's picture was different. It appeared to have been carefully cut from a magazine. Ray looked on the back and found that Darlene had penciled in the margin: "Allen, 4, '65." He took another look at the photo of the priest and suddenly recalled that after Darlene's funeral, he and his brothers had found this same picture in a small frame resting on a shelf in her kitchen. "Wonder what ever happened to that picture?" Ray said to himself.

On the bottom of the page were two small photo-booth snapshots of Darlene and what appeared to be the same priest, slightly older but in civilian clothes. The opposite, left-facing page contained individual and group pictures of all Darlene's brothers (including Ray), their sister Norma Jean, and their mother and father.

"She's got the whole family on this page," thought Ray. "But what's this priest doing here? Why did she have her picture taken with him in the photo booth? Why did Darlene cut out this little boy's picture and put it in between them? And what in the world is all this correspondence about an adoption?"

Ray was feeling both curious and a bit queasy as he turned the page.

There he saw a 1961 senior class picture of Darlene; a small, handmade birth announcement that said: "Bill Patrick, February 7, 1962, 7 lb. 8 oz., 20 in., 1:31 AM"; a shopping list with items that included "blanket," "gown," and "pacifier"; and an invoice, dated February 19, 1962, from "St. Anthony's Infant Home" of Kansas City. This invoice was made out to one "Janet Wheeler" in the amount of $369.35 for "Board," "Medicines and Miscellaneous Supplies," "Board after Delivery," and "Hospitalization" for the period between mid-September 1961 through late-February 1962.

Darlene had also included seven religious cards on that particular page. As Ray read the back of each card, he noted that the cards were carefully placed in chronological order. The first one was dated 1950, her first full year in the orphanage. On its front was a guardian angel looking over a sleeping child.

On the front of the seventh card was a beautiful picture of the Virgin Mary. On the back, written in his sister's handwriting, were the words: "Mother," "Darlene," "'62."

After reading that, Ray bolted upright as if he'd been shot in the back. Then he put the album down, walked into the bathroom and vomited.

Chapter Two

That afternoon, Ray called Gene, his younger brother, and told him he wanted to get all the brothers together. "I've got something to tell you all that'll shock you," he said.

"What's that?" asked Gene.

"It'll be better if I just tell all of you at the same time."

"Okay, I'll have everybody over here at seven o'clock tonight. Okay?"

"Yeah."

That evening, the Albert brothers gathered at Gene Albert's kitchen table. There was Roy, (age forty-six), Donald (forty-eight), the twins Gene and Dean (fifty) and, of course, Ray (fifty-four). Gene's wife, Esther, made sure they all had something to drink and then retired to another room to be with her mother.

"I want to show you something," said Ray as he placed Darlene's album on the table. "Have any of you ever seen this before?"

"No, what is it?"

"I found this scrapbook in some of Darlene's old boxes today," continued Ray. "I also found some papers that said she had a baby."

"No way," said Dean.

"C'mon, Raymond," piped in Roy. "Surely, that can't be true."

Ray then opened the album to the first page. "Well, see for yourself."

The brothers instantly recognized the orphanage class photograph.

"I remember when that picture was taken," said Gene. "It was the last one before we went to Boys Town. There's Father Wheeler and the nuns—and all of us. Look how young we looked."

"Hey, that's Father Mulvihill," remarked Dean as he pointed to the picture of the priest at the upper left. "He used to have Darlene over all the time to clean his house."

"You mean at the rectory?" asked Ray.

"Yeah."

"How old was she?"

"Gosh, she did that for years. Must have started when she was thirteen or fourteen years old."

Ray next proceeded to show his brothers the birth announcement, the shopping list, the invoice, the religious cards, and the letters from Catholic Charities and the Missouri Department of Health.

After a slight pause, Donald pointed toward the top three pictures. "Look here how Darlene put the picture of this little boy between her and Mulvihill."

"Do you guys remember when Mulvihill drove Darlene to Kansas City?" asked Ray.

"He did?"

"Yeah."

"When?"

"Right after she graduated from high school."

"That would have been in 1961."

"Why did he do that?"

"I thought it was just to further her education."

"She must have been pregnant."

"Yeah, it says on this invoice she was admitted to St. Anthony's Infant Home on September 12, 1961."

"But that's made out to Janet Wheeler."

"Who's Janet Wheeler?"

"Wonder if she's related to Father Wheeler?"

"Hell, guys, it was probably Darlene using a fictitious name."

[Silence]

"Did Norma Jean ever say anything about Darlene going to Kansas City? Weren't they living together back then?"

"Yeah, they were for a little while."

"Never said anything to me about it."

"You know, come to think of it, I do remember Norma Jean mentioning that she thought Darlene might be pregnant. When I asked her why, she said, 'Because her breasts were getting larger.'"

"Was that before or after she went to Kansas City?"

"Don't remember. Heck, it was more than thirty years ago."

[More silence]

"Well, I remember Mulvihill coming over to Henry's Tailor Shop a couple of times looking for Darlene. He was pretty agitated. Dressed in civilian clothes and smoking a cigar."

"What?"

"Yeah, he said she had moved and he didn't know where she was."

"What did you tell him?"

"I said I didn't know where she was."

"When was that?"

"I think it was in the summer. Probably August of '62."

"That would have been six months after she had the baby."

[More silence]

"You know, I remember back when I was delivering papers, I stopped by Mulvihill's house to drop off some books to Darlene because I knew she was there cleaning his house. But nobody answered the door."

"Maybe nobody was home."

"No. His car was parked outside and she told me she'd be there."

"Do you think they were having a relationship?"

"Well, *obviously* they were having a relationship."

"Wait a minute, now. Let's not jump to any conclusions."

"Come on, what the hell do you think was going on in there?"

"Well, I don't know."

"Look at this album. Mulvihill's the father of Darlene's baby!"

"Well, that's a pretty serious accusation. A priest and a young girl like that. We don't know for sure."

"Come on, Gene. Wake up."

"I just remembered something," said Donald. "Once, when Darlene was pretty drunk, she grabbed my arm and began sobbing. Said she had a baby by a priest."

"Oh, Christ. What did you say to her?"

"Nothing. I didn't know what to say."

[Silence]

"Listen, guys, I have something else to tell you," said Ray breaking the stillness.

"What?"

"Well, when I was in the orphanage, I had a sexual affair with a nun."

Incredulous, everyone just stared at Ray.

"It was Sister Agnesina. We slept together one night. Got caught. She was transferred out the next day."

"Jesus, Ray! How old were you?"

"Twelve."

"TWELVE!!!!!"

"Twelve???"

"It was in 1952. I threw up last night when I remembered what happened. It was like a flash of light going off. Darlene's religious cards made me remember that someone left three cards on my pillow that night. Can't believe I haven't thought about it in all these years."

"You must have put it out of your mind back when you were a kid."

[Silence]

"Well, I was molested by Father Wheeler on the trip up to Boys Town," said Roy out of nowhere.

Now everyone just stared at Roy.

"Huh?" asked Dean finally.

"Yeah, we were in the car and he put my hand on his . . . you know."

"He did that to me one time, too," confessed Gene.

"Me, too," said Donald.

"What about you, Dean," asked Ray. "You were in that car, too, weren't you."

"Yeah, but I was in the back seat the whole trip."

"So was I," recalled Gene. "But Father Wheeler also gave me a physical just before we left for Boys Town. Called me into his room, told me to drop my pants, and then felt my privates. That's all there was to the physical. I could tell he was hard."

"He did that to me, too," said Donald.

"Me, too," said Roy.

"Dean?" asked Ray.

"No."

"I was also molested by Sister Joachim," said Gene.

"What?!"

"Yeah, remember I had that bedwetting problem? Well, one day she . . ."

"Jesus Christ, do we have to talk about all this shit right now?" snapped Dean. "It's too much."

"Yeah, you're right," said Ray. "That's enough for one night."

"I just want to know one thing," said Donald. "How come nobody ever mentioned this stuff before? How come we never talked about it before?"

"Well, hell, I don't know. Maybe we blocked it out, too."

"Yeah. Besides, it's not the easiest thing in the world to discuss."

"I thought it just happened to me. I didn't know it happened to you guys, too."

[Silence]

"Man! Four out of five brothers. Darlene. Wonder if anything happened to Norma Jean?"

"Yeah, something happened to her, too. She mentioned it one time when she was drunk and out of it."

"What did she say?"

"Can't remember, exactly."

"Well, we can't ask her, now, can we."

"God rest her soul."

"Can't ask Darlene, either."

"Damn."

After one final prolonged pause, during which everybody was looking visibly shaken, Ray decided to break up the meeting.

"Let's call it a night, guys," he said. "I'm going home."

When Ray got back to his apartment, he grabbed a beer out of the refrigerator, turned on the television, and plopped himself down on the couch. He knew if he kept thinking about Darlene and what happened in the orphanage he wouldn't get much

sleep that night. He had to go to Hutchison early the next morning to open a new store—so he tried to focus in on the television.

But it was no use. His mind kept wandering. And his eyes
kept peering over at Darlene's album on the coffee table. After
taking a big gulp of beer, he finally picked it up and began
turning the pages.

Ray flipped though endless black-and-white photographs of
his brothers, his sisters, his parents, the family farm, the old
house, his grandparents. And his mind drifted back—back to the
days before the orphanage, before they were all taken away. Back
to the days when they were a real family—a mother, a father, and
nine children living in that little house on Fern Street.

Chapter Three

Rummaging through some old fruit crates behind the Safeway store, ten-year-old Ray Albert finally came upon a bunch of overripe bananas. "Look, here," he said to his brothers and sisters. "They threw these out! Can you believe it?"

With quiet deliberateness, Ray handed one banana each to Norma Jean, Darlene, and the twins, Gene and Dean—who immediately peeled back the skins and scarfed down the fruit inside. Then, having saved the last and smallest banana for himself, he leaned his back against the wall and wearily slid to the ground to savor each bite.

As the children began to traverse the few blocks back home, they passed row upon row of small saltbox houses, each separated by no more than three or four feet. And they playfully dodged between all the cars, which were parked on the streets because there were no garages in the neighborhood. Most of the autos were more than five or ten years old, some rusty and beat up. On this particular afternoon, Ray's attention was drawn to a 1949 Chevrolet that stood out like a shiny new penny. It looked exactly like the car his father owned—the one he wasn't allowed to touch or ride in. In fact, the only time any of his brothers and sisters had ever been in that car was when his five-year-old sister, Mary Ann, was sick and had to be taken to the doctor. And that time, only Mary Ann and the baby got to go.

After about ten or fifteen minutes, the children walked through the gate in the chain-link fence that surrounded the Albert home at 223 N. Fern. With its yellow wood siding and four white pillars on the front porch, the little three-bedroom house stood out brightly among all the others on the street. But Ray, always the last to walk through the gate, was hesitant to go in. Sometimes the place got so small for him that he just had to stay outside to take in a few extra breaths of solitary air. With nine kids packed into such a small space, the house could quickly become crowded. And for Ray, the older he got, the more crowded it became, because his mother gave birth to a new baby nearly every year since he was born. In addition to Norma Jean, age nine, Darlene (eight), Dean and Gene (six), and Mary Ann (five), there were also three younger brothers: Donald (four), Roy (two), and the four-month-old baby, Lonnie Lee.

Ray hardly spent any time with his mother, Clara, because it was all she could do just to keep up with the three little ones. And since his dad was rarely home, she expected him to take care of the other children. To Ray, it seemed like it had always been that way. "You need to be in charge of your brothers and sisters when I'm too busy," his mother had told him ever since he could remember. "You're the oldest. So be my little man."

Clara herself had come from a very large family. The tenth of fifteen children, and the only girl, she was constantly attending to her younger brothers. Overall, the elder Martin household was run with a heavy hand by parents who were staunchly Catholic and very strict when it came to the rules of everyday living. Her father had owned a farm in Oklahoma where Clara was born. But the family fell on hard times during the dust bowl years, sold off their property, and bought a smaller place near Wichita in the little farming community of Maize.

Clara was forced to quit school after the seventh grade and, for the next ten years, did little more than be a farmer's daughter—cooking, cleaning, and serving her father and brothers. In fact, she was rarely ever allowed to leave the place. But one autumn night in 1936, something happened that changed her life forever.

It was the Martins' turn to host a barn cleaning—a social event where all the farmers in and around Maize gathered to clean and spruce up each other's property. Afterwards, as was the custom, a barn dance was held to reward everyone for their hard day's work. It was there that Clara met a tall, good-looking young man from a farm about ten miles away. Joe Albert only had a sixth-grade education and was, for all intents and purposes, illiterate. But he was a bright lad with a sweet smile and attractive, deep-set brown eyes.

Joe had heard about Clara Martin, but because she rarely left the Martin property, he'd never had the opportunity to meet her. No one had. This night, though, he couldn't keep his eyes off her tall, striking figure leaning alone against the barn wall. He asked her to dance—and the two quickly became smitten with each other.

A few months later, Clara announced to her parents that she was going to marry Joe Albert. But the news was received less than favorably. The Alberts were farming riffraff, her father told her. And Joe, in particular, was a ne'er-do-well who couldn't read or write or hold down a job. She couldn't marry him, he said. She had to stay right there on the farm where she belonged. But on October 14, 1936, Clara packed her suitcase, eloped with Joe, and then moved in with his family—events that would forever create a rift between the Martins and the Alberts.

The first few years of their marriage were unsettling for Clara. Not only would her family not speak to her, but her father's warning seemed to be coming true as Joe constantly bounced from one job to another. Essentially, she stayed home, kept the house, and prayed for a child of her own. At last, after a little more than two years of waiting, she became pregnant and Raymond was born. Norma Jean arrived the next year, Darlene a year after that, and so on. By the time the ninth child, Lonnie Lee, was born on October 1, 1948, Joe was holding down a job as a baggage handler at the railroad station in downtown Wichita, and Clara and the children were firmly entrenched in the Fern Street house.

The more his family grew, the tougher it was for Joe to make ends meet. That, in turn, increased the tension between him and Clara—and Joe reacted by staying away as much as possible. Rather than going home after work, he would go out drinking with his buddies. Neighbors soon reported to Clara that they had seen her husband smoking big cigars while cruising around in his car. He also caroused with women at the downtown bars, they told her.

Because Joe usually drank his weekly paycheck, there was never enough money for Clara to run the household. She simply had to make do with whatever money she could squeeze out of him. Consequently, the Albert children were always poorly dressed, the house was usually a mess, and the refrigerator seemed to be forever barren of groceries.

But worst of all, Clara was often forced to decide which of her children were going to be fed and which weren't. There was, for instance, only one bottle of milk delivered on the front porch every morning—and that just wasn't enough to go around. But all of the kids needed milk, especially the young ones—Mary Ann, Donald, Roy, and Lonnie Lee.

Every day Clara had to answer the grim question: "Who will get the milk today?"

Chapter Four

When Ray woke up on the morning of January 28, 1949, he glanced over at his three brothers lying beside him. All the kids slept three or four to a bed, and Ray had to sleep with the younger boys so he could keep an eye on them at night. He could tell by the way they were breathing that Roy and Donald were still fast asleep. But Lonnie Lee, lying closest to him, was unusually still and cold to the touch.

Ray quickly got up and went into his parents' room.

"Mom, something's wrong with Lonnie."

Clara came in, picked up her motionless four-month-old and cradled him in her arms.

"Did you roll on top of him?" she asked Ray.

"No."

"My God, he's not breathing. Go get your father."

Joe came in and took a very close look at Lonnie Lee. Then he went next door to use the phone.

"Got to call the coroner," he said to his neighbor. "The baby died last night."

In a few minutes, the county coroner and an assistant showed up at the Albert residence. Joe showed them into the bedroom where Clara was still clinging to her baby. All the children were now also in the room and looking on intently.

After examining the baby for a few minutes, the coroner looked over at Joe and sadly shook his head.

Clara started sobbing uncontrollably and clutched Lonnie Lee ever tighter.

"Mrs. Albert, I'm going to have to take him now."

"No, no, no! He'll be all right! He'll be all right!"

"Clara," said Joe quietly, "let the doctor have Lonnie Lee."

The coroner's assistant placed a small black suitcase on the bed and opened it up. Then he put Lonnie Lee in the suitcase, closed it, picked it up, and started to leave.

"You're hurting him!" yelled one of the children. "Why are you putting him in there?"

"It's okay," said Joe. "The doctors have to take Lonnie Lee with them now."

As the men left, Ray went over and hugged his wailing mother. But she would not be consoled.

A week later, Joe walked into the house with a pick and shovel and told Clara that he was going over to the cemetery to dig a grave for Lonnie Lee. He had arranged for a burial site in the cemetery behind St. Mark's Catholic Church, he said, but could not find anyone willing to dig the grave on account of it being so cold outside. "Just as well," he said, "can't afford to pay anybody anyway."

"I'm going, too," said Ray, matter-of-factly. "I'm gonna help."

Joe paused for a moment to look at his oldest son.

"All right," he said, finally. "Get your coat on and let's go."

The sun was going down quickly when they arrived at the burial site—and Ray would never forget how really, really cold it was. The shovel could not break the hard ground, so Joe began by using the pick. With each swing, a big chunk of frozen dirt came up. Finally, he got far enough below the surface that Ray could help with the shovel. After they had dug several feet, Joe decided to stop.

"Is this deep enough?" asked Ray.

"I think they usually like it to be six feet, but this is just a little coffin. That'll do."

The next morning, Lonnie Lee's body was brought into the Albert house for a wake. Friends, neighbors, and family members all came to pay their respects. Clara's parents and brothers were all there. But sternly sullen and quiet, they refused to speak to Joe Albert. Around two o'clock everybody headed over to St.

Mark's for a short funeral mass. Afterwards, little Lonnie Lee was buried out back in a small wooden pauper's casket.

As Ray watched his brother's body being lowered into the four-foot-deep grave he had helped dig himself, he worried—worried about whether or not he might, indeed, have rolled over on the baby during the night. It would be another forty years before he would learn that the coroner had listed "malnutrition" as the cause of death.

Chapter Five

For six months after the death of Lonnie Lee, Stephen and Alphonse Martin kept a watchful eye on the comings and goings of Joe Albert and the situation in their older sister's house. They seemed to be more motivated by anger toward Joe than by concern for the children, because they never spoke to Clara nor offered her any financial help. Rather, while one occasionally cruised along Fern Street, the other would follow Joe around to "try and get something on him."

In mid-August, Alphonse noticed two Safeway employees chase off several of the children as they foraged for food at the back of store. The next day he went down and told county juvenile authorities about the incident and asked that an investigation be conducted into the well-being of the Albert children and the fitness of their father to provide for them. Alphonse was then informed that two neighbors of the Alberts had also filed complaints alleging inadequate food for the children and abuse of the mother by the father.

In response, county officials assigned the case to officer Mary Smith, who began a ten-day investigation. She interviewed the Safeway grocers and the neighbors who had complained—then she showed up at the Alberts' front door. There she met with Clara, Joe, all the children, and observed the entire situation first-hand. In her report, she described the house as "filthy," the children as "poorly dressed," and stated that "food was a problem" as the children were "undernourished."

Mrs. Smith then conveyed her findings to the Martin brothers, who agreed to support charges against Joe and Clara. But because Clara was their sister, they asked if the neighbors would be willing to sign the formal papers—which they were. So on August 25, 1949, Mrs. Rowena Loehr and Mrs. LaDean Luther, both ardent Catholics, filed a Petition for Dependent and Neglected Children stating:

> That said children . . . have idle and immoral habits—habitually beg and receive alms—suffer neglect, cruelty, or depravity on the part of their parents, in whose care said children are kept, in an unfit place for said children, in violation of the statutes of the State of Kansas . . . and against the dignity of Kansas.

As a result, later that day a squadron of policemen showed up at 223 N. Fern Street, arrested Joe and Clara, and took custody of all the children. The following morning, an article in *The Wichita Eagle* explained events in some detail:

> Parents of 8 Children Face Trial on Neglect Charges
>
> While Joseph Albert drove a 1949 model auto to a job that paid $300 per month, several of his eight children made a practice of snatching food from garbage cans, Mrs. Mary Threlfall Smith, county juvenile officer, charged Thursday when she issued a warrant against Albert and his wife, Clara.
>
> The Alberts were charged with contributing to the neglect and dependency of their children. The children, who range in age from 10 to 2, were taken to Wichita Children's Home. Mary Ann, 5, was taken from there directly to Wesley hospital; examining physicians found her seriously ill of a heart condition, the juvenile officer reported. The parents said the child had suffered from rheumatic fever, she added.
>
> Both Mr. and Mrs. Albert were put in the county jail Thursday afternoon but Probate Judge Clyde M. Hudson released the husband on $1,000 bond so he may continue to work. Mrs. Albert was held in jail pending the hearing in court, set for August 31.

At that hearing, all charges against Clara were dropped, but Joe was subsequently convicted of contributing to the "delinquency, dependency and neglect" of his children and sentenced to a year in the county jail and a fine of $1,000. The fine and sentence were suspended, however, on the conditions that he post a

$2,000 bond to the State of Kansas and "pay the sum of $15 per month per child support when said children are placed in a home other than his own." Joe also received the judge's stern warning that if the offense was committed again, the suspension would be voided and he would be sent to prison.

Clara, who had languished in the county jail for an entire week, left her husband and went back to live on the Martin farm. Joe moved out of the house and simply disappeared for a time. Meanwhile, all eight of the Albert children were officially declared wards of the court and scattered around the city of Wichita.

Donald and Roy were the only Albert kids to remain at the Wichita Children's Home. Five-year-old Mary Ann, suffering from malnutrition and a critical heart condition, was placed in the intensive care unit at Wesley Hospital. Norma Jean and Darlene were sent to a state home for girls called Friendly Gables, while Ray and the twins were transferred to Boys Farm, a criminal correctional reformatory. Being only six years old, Gene and Dean were allowed to stay in the minimum security section of the prison. But their older brother wasn't so fortunate.

On his first day, Ray was led down to the basement and locked in with about three dozen other boys. It was a cold, damp place with old cots lining the walls, a large shower and bathroom facility in the corner, and about a half dozen cells where they locked up the boys who got out of line.

When Ray walked in, he was immediately confronted by several older black kids. Thinking he was going to get beaten up, Ray put up his fists in a defensive posture.

"What are you in here for?" asked one of the boys.

"I don't know," said Ray, lowering his fists slightly.

"Well, then, you couldn't have done anything wrong," came the reassuring response.

"Relax, kid," said one of the other boys. "Things aren't so bad down here. Neither are most of the kids. But stay away from that one over there in the corner."

"Why?" asked Ray.

"Because he murdered his parents."

On the evening of September 4, 1949, there was a knock at the front door of the Martin family residence.

"Clara, someone's here for you," her father called out.

It was only four days after she was released from jail and ten days after all of the children were taken away. And now Clara Albert was notified by the social worker standing on the front porch that her daughter, Mary Ann, had died earlier that afternoon of complications from a heart condition.

"You never should have married that no-good Joe Albert," boomed her father, who then stalked off.

Stunned, Clara showed no emotion. She simply could not respond.

Turning away from the door, she walked slowly into the back living room where she picked up one of Mary Ann's dolls and sat down in a rocking chair facing the window. In less than a year, two of her children had died and the rest had been taken from her because they said she was an unfit mother.

In shock, Clara just sat there—rocking in her chair and staring out the window. Rocking and staring. Rocking and staring.

Chapter Six

The Martins may have hated Joe Albert, but after all that had happened to him—having his family taken away; being thrown in jail, humiliated in court, convicted of a crime; separating from his wife, enduring the death of two children—even they were amazed when he made a valiant effort to change his ways and reunite his family.

He stopped drinking, stopped prowling the bars at night, stopped carousing with women, even stopped smoking those big cigars. He also traded in his new Chevrolet for a less expensive used car and then went out and got himself a second job at night. Joe's goal was to earn enough money to get his entire family back together by Christmas—a pretty tall order to accomplish in less than four months, but he was determined to make it happen.

And sure enough, when December rolled around, Joe called Clara to tell her that he had just placed a down payment on a house in Goddard. Would she move there with him if they could get the kids back? She responded that she would. Together, then, Joe and Clara petitioned the court for the return of their seven children.

On December 20, 1949, a formal hearing was held to consider the matter. Joe was present, but Clara stayed home. Impressed with the father's apparent resolve to turn things around, and probably feeling the spirit of the season, the presiding judge agreed to return the Albert children to their parents on a trial basis. But he further asserted that the children were official wards of the court, that they were still viewed as dependent and neglected, and that strict terms of probation must be met.

Energized and euphoric, Joe left the courthouse and drove straight to the Martin family farm where he picked up Clara amid the stares and glares of her parents and brothers. He then drove her about ten miles west of Wichita to the little town of Goddard and showed her their new house. Together, they spent the rest of the day cleaning, moving furniture, shopping, filling the refrigerator and cupboards with food—generally readying the place for their children.

It took Joe most of the next day to pick up everybody and return them home. First, he went to Friendly Gables for Darlene and Norma Jean, who were packed and eagerly waiting for him at the front entrance. Then, after driving the girls to Goddard, he headed over to the Wichita Children's Home to get Roy and Donald. The administrators there carefully and deliberately verified all the court papers and confirmed his identification as the father. After several hours, the youngsters were finally handed over to him.

Now figuring that it might take quite awhile to secure the release of his older sons, Joe drove Donald and Roy home and then made his final trip back to Wichita. He found the people at Boys Farm disorganized, unprepared, and actually not expecting him at all. But Joe had all the necessary documents—and he was polite and patient with the officials at the reformatory. He had made up his mind that he would do almost anything to get the boys out of that hellhole—and he wasn't going to leave until he had them.

At last, Gene and Dean came out with bundles of clothes tucked under their arms. Clearly happy to be getting out, they ran to their dad and hugged him. Ray, on the other hand, was considerably withdrawn when he emerged about a half hour later. He merely looked at his father and nodded. It had been a tough four months.

On the way home, the twins chatted excitedly while Ray sat silently in the front seat. As the car approached the corner of First and Goddard streets, the boys saw the little white house where they were now going to live. Resting on a quarter of an acre, it was more out in the country than the previous home. There were a few other houses nearby, but there wasn't any traffic on the streets to speak of. In the yard were a couple of bird feeders, a birdbath, and lots of trees—maples, spruces, a few evergreens, and a big weeping willow in the front.

As soon as they pulled into the driveway, Clara and the other children ran out the door to greet them. While Donald and Roy rushed into their mother's arms, Ray stood to the side and looked skyward for a moment. He was captivated by the beautiful color contrast between the green leaves on the trees and the deep blue of the vast Kansas sky.

"Maybe this won't be so bad," he thought to himself.

Chapter Seven

Things were pretty good for awhile. Christmas was filled with presents, food, good cheer, and best of all, the family was together. After the holidays, Clara and the kids settled into a new routine—with new schools and new friends. And twice a month, without exception, juvenile officer Mary Smith made scheduled visits to the Albert home. Clara and Joe were always prepared when she showed up, too. The house was clean, the refrigerator filled, and all the children were on their best behavior.

Although everything seemed fine, Clara's brothers were still keeping a close eye on the situation. Their hostility toward Joe Albert had increased when he'd persuaded Clara to leave with him again. They wanted her at home where she belonged—and that was that. So they reported any little perceived problem or violation to the authorities.

Unfortunately, the Albert home situation never really got to where everything was great. After a few months, the kids again weren't getting enough food to eat. And Joe wandered out to the bars once in awhile. His carousing wasn't as bad as before, but the Martin brothers quickly reported his behavior.

As a result, in March, Mary Smith paid a surprise visit to the little house in Goddard. This time, she found the kids poorly dressed, the house a mess, and not much food around. In private, she asked the children if they were hungry. Several answered yes, and one even said, "I'm always hungry."

The next day, Mary Smith made out her report and determined that the Alberts were simply not capable of taking proper care of their children. Everything boiled down to the sad fact that there were just too many mouths to feed. Even holding down two jobs, Joe Albert simply could not make ends meet.

But Mrs. Smith was worried about the ultimate welfare of the seven children. So she called the Martins and informed them that she was willing to recommend that the kids be removed from the home again, but expressed serious concern about sending them to state-sponsored institutions. "They might be better off with their parents than in these homes," she said, "especially the boys who could end up going back to Boys Farm."

The Martins immediately appealed to the Catholic Diocese of Wichita to get involved and assume responsibility for the children. Church officials were only too happy to comply, because the Martin family was a big financial contributor to their diocese. Besides, they were always on the lookout for kids to fill up their children's home in El Dorado. And the prospect of receiving seven children from one family immediately drew their attention.

On March 22, 1950, almost exactly three months after Joe Albert had regained temporary custody of his children, a new hearing was conducted in Sedgwick County Court. Joe, Mary Smith, and representatives from the Wichita Catholic Diocese were present. Clara stayed at home with two-year-old Roy (who was sick with the flu), and the other Martins did not show up.

Joe Albert made a heartfelt plea to keep his older children. "We can handle them, at least," he said. "You know we can."

But both County and Church officials fought against it—arguing that the kids would be better off with the Sisters of St. Joseph in the El Dorado children's home. At least there, they'd receive ample food, clothing, schooling, and medical care. Besides, they said, the children would be together as family. And that was better than splitting them apart.

After all sides were heard, the Albert children were again adjudicated wards of the court and ordered taken from their parents. The judge then officially placed all seven "into the care, custody, dominion, and control of the Catholic Church in Wichita, Kansas, pending further order of this Court."

Two days later, on Friday, March 24, 1950, Joe Albert loaded six of his seven kids into his car and drove them to Wichita. Roy was allowed to stay with Clara until his health improved.

Ray recalled his mother standing on the front porch looking "about as sad as a person could possibly look." And he would carry that picture, that moment, and that sinking feeling with him for the rest of his life.

Barely a word was said on the ride into town. "They're going to take you to El Dorado," was all Joe told his children. "But why?" asked Ray. His father did not respond.

Joe drove to the Wichita Courthouse where he met Mrs. Smith. Without speaking to her, he transferred all the kids' bags to the trunk of her car and turned to his children. "You all go with her now," he said to them. "I'll see you later." Then he got in his car and drove away.

Forty-five minutes later, Mary Smith pulled her car up in front of the St. Joseph Home for Children in El Dorado, Kansas. The seven Albert kids piled out of the car and stared at the large, imposing, red brick structure. It was the biggest building some of them had ever seen. Up the steps and through the big door they walked—all the while staying close together, as close as possible. Waiting inside were a priest and two nuns.

"Welcome, children," said Father Michael R. Blackledge. "We are pleased to have you with us. Sister Charles and Sister Joachim will now show you to your rooms."

As the priest turned and began to walk down the hallway, one of the nuns opened a stairwell door and motioned for the children to move through.

"Why are we here?" Ray asked the nun.

"I don't know," she replied.

"Yes you do! I want to know! Why are we here?"

"Come along, young man," said the other nun.

But Ray ran after the priest instead. "Father," he said, "why are we here?"

The priest stopped for a moment and looked down at the tearful ten-year-old. But saying nothing, he turned away and resumed his walk down the hall.

"Why won't you tell me?" screamed Ray. "Why are we here? Why? Why? Why?"

From this point on, the Albert children were totally dependent and reliant upon the Catholic church for their care, their safety, and their well-being.

Chapter Eight

Father Michael R. Blackledge, an Englishman ordained in Ireland in late 1949, immigrated to Kansas in January, 1950, and was immediately assigned to the St. Joseph Home for Children in El Dorado. He had been there less than three months when the Albert children arrived.

Specifically requested by the Wichita diocese, Blackledge was the first of at least twenty-five Irish-ordained priests to arrive in Wichita in the decade of the 1950s. Prior to that influx, the diocese had never received more than three priests from Ireland in any given decade since the turn of the century. A major reason for the increase was related to social living conditions prevalent in Ireland at the time.

The Catholic church was a big part of Irish life—so much so that it was actually written into the nation's constitution. Due to the church's decree that contraception was not allowed in any form, families tended to be very large. It was not uncommon, for instance, to see ten, twelve, even fourteen or more children in a single household. On top of that, every Irish mother wanted at least one of her sons to become a priest. And because Ireland had a terrible economy with most families languishing in poverty, the priesthood was seen as a legitimate profession—a way out of an endless cycle of depression and destitution.

The government of Ireland also offered formal schooling at a variety of institutions similar to the famous Manuthe Seminary located on the edge of Dublin. There, with all their expenses paid, young men were trained for the priesthood. Among other things, they were taught how the Catholic church was run, what their relationship to parishioners should be, and that the role of the church in society was superior.

As the population of Ireland grew, so did the oversupply of priests. There simply weren't enough parishes in the tiny nation to take them all. So the Catholic church shipped these young clergymen all over the world—to other parts of Europe, Asia, South America, and Australia. But the nation receiving the largest number of Irish-born priests, by far, was the United States. As a result, America's Catholic church was very heavily influenced by the practices and culture of the Irish Catholic church. Obviously, then, by the time they were given sole custody of the Albert children, the Wichita diocese was already impacted by that cultural influence—and, as more and more Irish priests arrived each year, it became even more deeply entrenched.

And what were Ireland's methods in dealing with young children who were adjudicated wards of the state?

First of all, it's important to realize that many large Irish families lived in squalor, in part because the parents were overwhelmingly poor and unskilled. Not only was there no access to family planning or contraception, but abortion was a criminal offense. So there were, literally, thousands of unsupervised children running around all over the place—in every small village and hamlet, in every large urban area.

Forced to confront the problem, the Irish government passed laws stating that children could be arrested and sentenced for the crimes of "being found wandering," "being illegitimate," or "having an inability to show proper guardianship." Also, women who practiced prostitution, or were otherwise judged to be promiscuous, could have their children taken away on the grounds of "endangering the morality of children."

As a result, children from the ages of a few weeks up to eighteen years of age were picked up off the streets, or forcibly removed from their parents' custody, and then placed into government/Catholic-run orphanages called "industrial schools." And by 1949, there were more than six thousand children held in forty-five of these institutions across Ireland—ostensibly to be cared for, rehabilitated, and trained for some useful vocation.

But the truth is that there was very little training, rehabilitation, or care in any of these so-called "industrial schools." In reality, they were run more like prisons. The children, often referred to as "inmates," were forced to work without compensation in laundries, on farms, and in small factories. The government dictated what they ate ("plain, wholesome food"), how long they played ("two hours a day"), how long they worked, and how long they went to school. In most cases, the government of Ireland paid various Catholic religious orders, such as a diocese, convent, or monastery, to run the institutions and watch over the children.

A common rule among nuns, brothers, and priests was to stress discipline over kindness. But many times authority turned deliberately harsh and cruel. Over the years, stories have emerged of violent beatings, intense mental anguish, and ongoing sexual abuse. Some children, for instance, were forced to thread beads on a wire for hours on end to make rosaries for nuns who beat them savagely if they made a mistake. Boys habitually seemed to be abused more than girls. They were beaten more frequently and savagely by the nuns, and they were more often the victims of homosexual abuse and pedophilia. As a result, they were always trying to escape.

A 1959 government report on the Letterfrack industrial school in County Galway (which was run by the Christian Brothers religious order) referred to recurrent "breakouts." "Since Christmas, eleven boys ran away at different times," noted the February report. Problem boys who attempted to "break out" were then often transferred around from institution to institution until they were sixteen years old and, hence, eligible to enter military service or be "deported" to England.

Some internal reports at Letterfrack also focused on the financial viability of the institution. Words like "income," "expenditures," "deficits," and "profits," were used repeatedly. Because Ireland's Department of Education provided a stipend for each child at the institution, "profitability" depended, to a very large degree, on the number of children held. As a result, some reports referred to obtaining as many as possible of "these children who mean so much financially to the institution"—and being "ever on the lookout for boys" to be secured. One report also specifically credited a reversal in declining numbers "owing to the fact that one of the Dublin judges frequently sends convicted boys" to the orphanage.

In the early 1950s, at nearly the same time the Albert children were deposited in El Dorado, Kansas, a young Irish girl named Patricia O'Connor and her four brothers were loaded into a van and taken forcibly from their home in Dublin, Ireland, by the St. Vincent de Paul Catholic charity. After being adjudicated in a local metropolitan district court, they were then committed to Dublin's Goldenbridge Children's Home. Patricia and her brothers were not told why they were taken from their parents, nor did they ever live with them again.

Most of the Irish children in their situation were not told anything as to why they were ripped away from their parents and placed in an institution—either that or they were lied to about it. Some were eventually informed that their parents were dead and that they were orphans—when, in fact, their parents were still living, still married, and desperately wanted their children back.

Chapter Nine

Those children born to legally married parents, and subsequently taken into custody, were dubbed "legitimate" orphans by both the Irish government and Catholic church. *Illegitimate* babies, on the other hand, were a completely different matter—and in the decade of the 1950s, part of a completely different process.

First of all, the Irish government did not get involved in dealing with unwed pregnant girls. In that area, the Catholic church was solely in charge, because a young girl becoming pregnant before marriage was the worst sin possible—the "highest moral transgression" aside from murder. In Ireland, it was simply unspeakable to have a child out of wedlock.

Unfortunately, because dancing and courting were such prevalent Irish leisure activities, many extended families experienced one of their daughters becoming pregnant before marriage. And these young women were, subsequently, treated horribly. They were shamed and shunned, their lives made insufferable by the very communities in which they lived. People whispered about them behind their backs. Friends and family abandoned them. And they were formally denounced by priests from the church pulpit at Sunday morning masses. In addition, because abortion was illegal, they were forced to have their babies. There was just no other option.

When a girl was found to be pregnant, her parents often tried to hide her from view. Others were beaten by their fathers, thrown out of the house, and disowned. Many pregnant girls, some as young as fourteen years old, were children themselves and had only one place to turn—the nearest institution catering specifically to women in their position.

Because premarital pregnancies were so widespread, "maternity" or "infant" homes run exclusively by the Catholic church sprung up all over Ireland. There were homes in Castlepollard, Cork, County Leitrim, and County Tipperary. There were several in the major urban area of Dublin—most notably, the St. Patrick's Guild, which actually doubled as both a home and an adoption society. And then there was the famous Magdalen Home in Galway run by the Sisters of Charity. This particular asylum was commonly called the Magdalen "Laundry"—referring to the prevailing kind of work women were forced to perform while there.

When a young woman arrived at the Magdalen Home, she was immediately given a number and a false name in order to shroud her identity in secrecy. No other "inmate" in the home would know who she really was. She was not free to leave, nor even allowed to venture off the grounds. All her mail was read prior to her receiving it—if she received any at all. She was perpetually tormented by unkind nuns for her "mortal sin" of becoming pregnant out of wedlock. And she was forced to work, and work hard, in order to pay for her room and board.

Every morning, the girls got up at 5:30 AM and went to a 6:00 AM mass. Then they started jobs which ranged from scrubbing the floors and bathrooms, to doing the laundry, to working in the nursery. It was the pregnant women who tended to newborn babies that were lined up in row upon row of cribs in room after room. Those infants were the lucky ones because many others did not survive childbirth. Babies who died were buried in shallow graves on church property without ever having been given a name. And due to the high infant mortality rate in the mid-twentieth century, there are literally hundreds of unnamed babies buried all over Ireland in the graveyards similar to the one at Sean Ross Abbey in Roscrea, County Tipperary.

After a girl had her baby, she was allowed to keep the child with her almost all day for up to a week—giving up the child only at night. She was also able to be present and hold her baby for its baptism ceremony. But once the new mother was back on her feet, she was forced to go back to work at the home in order to pay for the ongoing upkeep of her child. And whatever paltry wages she was paid were used to purchase baby clothing, blankets, and wash towels.

Compelling the girls to go back to work also served to start a gradual weaning of the child—not just from breast feeding, but from total contact with the mother. First, the hours per day they could spend together were cut from three one-hour sessions to two—and then finally mother and child were allowed to spend only one hour a day with each other. That hour always occurred in daylight while visitors "shopping" for babies sometimes looked on.

About a month after giving birth, the new mothers were forced to relinquish all legal rights to their babies. They were sent by the nuns to the offices of a local notary public, where they had to swear an oath and formally sign what was then commonly known as the "relinquishment form," or "document of surrender." Among other things, it stated: "I hereby relinquish full claim forever to my child . . . and I hereby surrender the said child . . . and I understand never to make any claim to the said child."

Young, frightened, and confused, many girls who signed away their rights were often coerced into doing so by both church officials and notaries who were paid a fee for each child that was "signed up." Afterwards, the girls returned to the asylum to continue their routine until a formal adoption took place.

After the passage of Ireland's Adoption Act of 1952, which allowed illegitimate children to be placed out for adoption, selling babies became a big business for the Irish Catholic church. Thousands born to unwed mothers were routinely sold, packaged, and shipped around the world through local and international adoption agencies. Some investigators estimate that more than forty thousand Irish children were sent abroad between 1955 and 1995 as part of this process. And, like the oversupply of Irish priests who were shipped out by the Catholic church, the greatest number of illegitimate babies, by far, were sent to the United States of America.

There were clauses included in the 1952 Adoption Act stating that the adoptive parents must be "of the same religion as the child and his parents or, if the child is illegitimate, his mother"— and that "a child's rights in respect of faith and morals must be protected by such safeguards as will assure his adoption by persons who profess the religion of the child." In other words, they had to be Catholic—and good Catholics, at that.

Accordingly, all prospective parents were carefully screened for their "suitability" and "commitment" to raising the child in the Catholic faith. Medical certificates had to be produced attesting to their general mental and physical health, and their home approved with an on-site inspection. In addition, all adoptive parents had to swear that they were "not deliberately shirking natural conception." They had to promise to bring the child up in the Catholic faith and educate him in Catholic schools. The mother had to promise to give up work outside the home. And both parents were required to sign a form imposing the condition that "there should be no publicity at any stage in connection with the adoption." In other words, they were sworn to secrecy.

After being approved by the adoption agency, the adoptive parents then had to write checks to cover all expenses—including air travel for the child, related paperwork for the adoption, fees for the agency, and a fee for the Irish Catholic church itself, which was usually two hundred pounds. Finally, the children were flown out of Ireland—usually on Pan Am airlines. "Please book your transportation at your Pan American office," wrote a nun in Dublin to prospective parents in Chicago. "All our children travel thus. We group them in four, and four adopting parents share the expenses of one guardian for the children."

It was not unusual for Pan Am flight manifests from Dublin to the United States to read: "Stewardess x 2 x 10%." Everyone associated with the airline knew that a "10 percent" was an Irish baby. And yet, despite the attempts at secrecy, it was not uncommon for people to approach Pan Am personnel in an effort to secure an adoption. One airline employee, for instance, recalled being approached at the Dublin flight counter by an American officer in uniform. "I'm back again," he said good-naturedly. "My wife was thrilled with the adopted daughter I brought her. Now I've come to buy myself a son." Forty years later, many adoptees who were finally able to learn the specifics of their adoptions would comment to each other that they "were born in the belly of a Pan Am jet."

The average time babies stayed with their mothers was six months. However, many mothers were forced to surrender children as old as two years—which was extraordinarily traumatic for both. Compounding the situation was the short notice given when an adoption finally came through.

"One day, just before Christmas, I came in to see my child and the nun told me to say goodbye," recalled one Irish woman some forty years later. When she saw her two-year-old daughter dressed in a new pink outfit and ready to travel, the mother began to weep. "Why are you crying?" asked the nun coldly. "Just say goodbye!" So she kissed her daughter goodbye and they took her away.

Many children were literally ripped from their mothers' arms kicking and screaming. If that happened too often, the next young girl might walk into the nursery expecting to see her child but, instead, be greeted with the horrifying words: "She's gone." To top it all off, birth mothers were not permitted to know where their children were being taken. They never knew that their babies were being sent thousands of miles away to America, Australia, or some other foreign land.

After the adoption took place, the girls were free to leave. Up to that point, however, they were not allowed to return to their old lives. And, unfortunately, the longer they stayed with their children, the harder it was to transition back to the real world—especially since they had little money, no job, and families who would not take them back. Many of the young women stayed in the vicinity of the asylum, taking jobs arranged by the nuns, and then eventually marrying and having more children. But some women never left the institution.

A sad story surfaced in 1997 of one such woman who died in the Magdalen Laundry in County Cork. As a pregnant teenage girl in 1952, she had been thrown out of her home by puritanical parents and secretly taken to the Home late at night. After her baby was born and adopted, her family would not take her back, so she stayed on as an unpaid worker because she had no place else to go. When she died in the mid-1990s, a nun contacted her surviving sister to make funeral arrangements. After an agreement was reached, the woman's body was removed from the asylum (now a convent) late at night, in secrecy, and quietly interred in the family plot. She had left the place exactly the same way she had arrived and was finally reunited with her family in death.

The separation of mother and illegitimate child was seen by the Catholic church as a clean answer to a moral dilemma. But the long-term effects on the mothers were never considered. Most women who went through it, left alone to grieve and wonder, remained scarred for life. Many pushed the pain way down, refused to talk about it, and became reclusive.

One woman, for years afterward, traveled to a nearby children's home, stood on the street outside, and watched the children at play in the courtyard—wondering if one of them was the son she had given up. Another searched crowds of people for the rest of her life—hoping beyond hope to recognize her long lost daughter.

First page of Darlene Albert's "secret" photo album

Joe and Clara Albert

Michael and Mary Martin,
Clara's Parents

Mary Ann Albert

The St. Joseph Home For Children in El Dorado, Kansas

Joe Albert visits his children at the Home

Girl's dormitory at the St. Joseph Home

Sister Charles in the Home's basement laundry

Joe Albert and sons at Boys Town
(clockwise from upper left:
Dean, Joe, Gene, Roy, and Donald

Bishop of the Wichita
Diocese, Mark Carroll, with
Cub Scouts (Donald Albert
is at left.)

Classroom at St. John's parochial school in El Dorado

Sisters of St. Joseph Order at the Home for Children

Right: Ray Albert as a Boy Scout, age 12

Below: Priests and nuns from the Catholic Diocese of Wichita

Top: Father William A. Wheeler with little Joe Kaiser in plaid shirt on his right

Right: Joe Kaiser as an angel in the Home's Christmas pageant

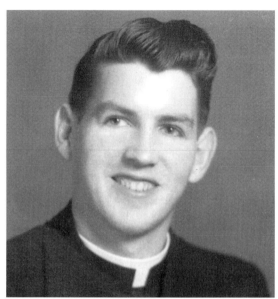

Father Daniel B. Mulvihill, age 27

Darlene Albert, 1958, age 16

Darlene Albert as the May Crowning Queen of St. John's Parish.
Surrounded by brothers (clockwise from upper left) Gene, Dean,
Roy, and Donald

Darlene Albert (left)
and sister Norma
Jean Albert, 1959

Darlene, the summer after her graduation

Darlene Albert's high school
graduation picture, 1961

Above: St. Anthony's Infant Home in Kansas City, Missouri

Below: Darlene's invoice statement from St. Anthony's Infant Home

STATEMENT

FROM   St. Anthony's Infant Home

        1414 E. 27th St.

        Kansas City, Mo.   Feb. 19   19 62

TO   Janet Wheeler   *Sister Mathilde*

ADDRESS 840 N. Topeka   *Morano*   *652*

CITY   Maize, Kansas   *816 BA1-7191*

TERMS

Board 9/12/61 - 10/10/61	$60.00	
Board 12/10/61 - 2/7/62	$126.45	
Medicines and Miscellaneous		
supplies	20.00	
	$206.45	
Board after Delivery		
2/14/62 - 2/20/62		
6 days	12.90	
Total Board Due	$219.35	
Hospitalization	$150.00	
Total Amount Due	$369.35	

Darlene and Father Daniel B. Mulvihill in Wichita photo booth,
August 1962

HAVING A HUSBAND

*Having a husband is diverse
with fat and lean, with better and worse,
with thick and thin, and trick and treat,
and taking the bitter with the sweet.*

*Having a husband is comforting, warm
as a summer wave. It's a cloud, a storm!
It's a rock on which you can depend
and a child for whom you have to fend!*

*It's shoulder to shoulder and side by side;
it's at opposite poles and against the tide;
it's a constant climate, a fickle weather
that can only be joined by two together!*
—HELEN HARRINGTON

7 lb. 8 oy'
20 in

Slickman
+
Miriane

Prayer card given to Darlene
upon leaving the Infant Home

On the back, she wrote:
"Mother. Darlene '62."

Darlene's hand-made birth
announcement for "Bill Patrick"

Photo booth picture of Tom Groetken on his wedding day, May 17, 1974

Photo booth picture of Darlene with dog, Tequila, on her wedding day, May 17, 1974

Tom Groetken and Darlene Albert at Eddie's Bar, Wichita, circa 1968

Dean and Norma, 1985

Back (L-R): Don, Norma, Ray; Front: Roy
1983

Chapter Ten

In search of her heritage, thirty-six-year-old Mary Ellen Hammer of Wichita, Kansas, walked into Dublin's St. Patrick's Institute in the spring of 1987. All she knew was what her father had told her—that she was born somewhere in Ireland in 1951 and had been sent to Kansas via an arranged adoption in 1952. An initial research contact told her that Dublin would be a good place to start, but the nuns at St. Patrick's had no information. So they referred her to the nearby Sisters of Charity, who had arranged thousands of adoptions in the '50s and '60s. Any records that may have survived would be there, they told her.

Mary Ellen's next meeting was with Sister Gabriel (of the Sisters of Charity) who politely, but firmly, stated that she could be of no help—even though records of her adoption might very well be in their files. "Our contract is not with you, it is with your mother," said the nun. "We cannot breach that confidentiality. Your mother would have to request a search in order for us to get involved."

Unable to get anywhere in Ireland, Mary Ellen returned to America to continue her research. But she was constantly stonewalled, thwarted, and given the runaround by officials of the Catholic church. Undaunted, she turned to a network of adoptees from whom she learned that many others had also tried and failed to locate their Irish birth mothers. A few had actually been able to gain access to some records but found key dates and names altered—apparently in a bid to prevent tracing of the natural mothers. Others found that no records existed at all—having either been destroyed or never properly kept.

Finally, after nine years of frustration, Mary Ellen made the acquaintance of a compassionate and well-connected Irish chaplain who agreed to help her. Through some friends in Belfast, he was able to gain access to her records, contact her relatives in Ireland, and locate her birth mother.

It seems Mary Ellen's natural mother was one Kathleen Quinn who, finding herself pregnant at the age of sixteen, had entered the maternity home in Castlepollard, County West-meath in April of 1951. Born in the fall of that year, Mary Ellen was originally christened with the name Rosaleen. But six months later, her mother kissed her goodbye for the last time. Dressed in a pink outfit, she was put on a Pan Am jet with two baby boys (clothed in blue), flown across the Atlantic, and deliv-ered to her new parents, Marie and Melvin Hammer, in Wichita. As fate would have it, Kathleen Quinn had immigrated to the United States in 1958, married, and was living in New York. There, more than thirty years after they were separated, mother and child had a heartfelt, tearful reunion.

Afterwards, Mary Ellen threw a thank-you party for the Kan-sas priest who had arranged her adoption—along with twenty others in the Wichita area back in the '50s. It seems this particu-lar Catholic clergyman had a key connection in Ireland—his sis-ter, who was a nun with the Sisters of Charity.

That priest was Father Michael R. Blackledge.

Father Blackledge, who had left his position at the Children's Home in El Dorado about a month after the seven Albert children arrived, was reassigned to a parish in order to help fill openings created by a phenomenal expansion of the Catholic Diocese of Wichita. This growth was spurred on by the leadership of Bishop Mark Carroll who, upon taking over in 1947, immediately launched plans for a plethora of new churches, rectories, schools, convents, community centers, and hospitals. About this time, the Catholic church in the United States (taking its cue from Ireland) was setting up, among other church facilities, "institutions" to deal with unwed young women and orphans. In all, from 1947 to 1962, more than 180 new church buildings were erected in the Wichita metropolitan area—and the Catholic population increased by a staggering 56 percent.

As the diocese grew, so did the need for priests and nuns to staff the new buildings and minister to the increasing number of parishioners. So Bishop Carroll, who had sole authority to admit priests and nuns to his diocese, put out a call to the international Catholic church for help. For new nuns, the Sisters of St. Joseph, who'd maintained a presence in Wichita since the turn of the century, were extremely helpful in recruiting and securing additional members to help serve the Diocese. And in searching for available priests, Bishop Carroll quite naturally turned to the place where they were most abundant—the nation of Ireland.

Almost immediately, young Irish priests descended upon Kansas to have a look-see and determine if they wanted to "sign up." Most were favorably impressed with Wichita because it was more urban than rural—and because it was obviously a growing Catholic community. Wichita was viewed as a city on the rise, and consequently, opportunity and excitement beckoned.

And so, to Wichita, Kansas, came the Irish priests. From the rural country settings they came—from County Roscommon, County Clare, County Kerry, and County Mayo. From the sprawling urban cities they came—from Dublin, from Galway, from Carlow, Waterford, and Kilkenny. At least twenty-five in all arrived in the decade of the 1950s—each newly ordained and in his twenties—full of energy, full of vim and vigor, full of high hopes and grand expectations.

To Kansas they came. And with them came Ireland itself.

Chapter Eleven

"This way, boys," said Sister Charles as she opened the stairwell door to the second floor of the St. Joseph Home for Children.

"Girls, you come with me," beckoned Sister Joachim to Darlene and Norma Jean. "You'll be on the third floor."

As his sisters continued up the stairs, Ray led his brothers through the door and into the long, chilly corridor—which seemed unusually large and scary to the boys. On the walls, five feet up from the floor, were smooth yellow bricks the size of cinder blocks; the floor was government-issue hard tile; the high ceiling was lined with various sizes of pipes. Sister Charles walked at a brisk clip ahead of Ray and the others who lagged behind, their eyes darting around apprehensively. "Come along, boys," she urged, "come along."

On the left side of the hallway was one large bathroom facility with showers, wash basins, and toilets. On the right were four dormitory-type rooms. In each were ten metal beds lined up five on a side—headboards against the wall; footboards extending out to the aisle in the center of the room. Each bed was covered with a plain green military-style blanket. The boys were assigned to rooms by age. Ray was put in the room with ten- to twelve-year-olds. The twins, Dean and Gene, were in with boys six to nine. And Donald was placed with those five and younger.

Upstairs, the girls found the same general layout with two minor differences: only three rooms were being utilized, because there were fewer girls than boys in the home; and their beds were covered with nice patterned bedspreads. Fortunately, because Norma Jean and Darlene were only one year apart in age, they were assigned to the same room with beds right next to each other—and that made them happy.

A dozen nuns also lived at the home. Almost all of them had private rooms on the second floor—down the hall and on the other side of the building from the boys. A folding partition in the corridor separated the sisters' quarters from those of the children. The mother superior lived on the third floor with the girls. Only about five or six sisters were assigned permanently to the home as their regular "mission." The rest served temporarily and were transferred in and out on a regular, rotating basis. Most were members of the Sisters of St. Joseph order.

There was also one priest who lived at the home. In 1950, it was Father Blackledge—although there had been three before him and five others to follow. He had a private, two-bedroom apartment out back that was attached to the building by an elevated outside walkway. In effect, the chaplain (his official title) served as leader and ultimate authority at the Home. Just as in the Catholic church everywhere, the nuns answered to the priests— even though, in many cases, the women were more educated, more informed, and certainly closer to the children. The sisters were not allowed decision-making authority in the Church because they were not ordained. It was as simple as that.

Things were pretty quiet that first day. While Donald immediately went in with the preschoolers, the older children had a quiet lunch, explored the grounds, and played outside a bit. Around 3:30 PM, the other children began returning from school—first those in first to sixth grades and then the seventh and eighth graders. When the children graduated from the eighth grade they were placed in foster homes.

By 4:30, all seventy children were back in the orphanage, and the place came alive with activity. Ray was surprised at how many of the kids were related to each other. It seems that entire families of children had been taken out of their homes just like he and his brothers and sisters had been. There were the six Martinez kids, the four Greene brothers, and at least nine or ten groups of two to three siblings.

The Alberts, Ray later learned, were the largest family ever to enter the orphanage. But even if he had known that bit of trivia at the time, it really wouldn't have mattered to him. All he knew back then was that they were now grouped in with all the other kids there. And starting the next day, when they went to school for the first time, each would forever be known as one of the "Home" children.

Chapter Twelve

That first night was an uneasy one for the Albert kids—new bed, new place, new people, not knowing for sure what was going to happen the next day. None of them slept really well. But Ray was especially anxious and restless. He worried about his little brothers and sisters, wondered if he could somehow get a job so he could buy a house and support them all. How could his father have let this happen to them? How was his mother doing? All night long, Ray lay awake and fretted.

Then at 5:30 in the morning he heard some faint noises down the hall. Getting up to see what was going on, he walked out of his room, down the hall, and peeked through the partition where the noise was coming from. The nuns were bustling back and forth across the hallway. "It's real early," he thought to himself. "Still dark out. Wonder what they're doing."

He found out thirty minutes later when Sister Charles walked into his room and flipped on the light switch.

"Six o'clock!" she announced. "Good morning! Good morning! Everybody up!"

Suddenly, lights were going on everywhere and nuns were scurrying all over the place. It was the beginning of a new day at the orphanage—and the start of a daily routine that would not be altered, even one iota, for years.

Every school weekday it was the same: Get up at 6:00, make your bed, wash, dress, go down to the chapel on the first floor. Mass at 6:30. Pray. 6:45, do your little chore. Go down and work in the kitchen or the laundry, get things ready for breakfast, set the tables, sort the dirty clothes—whatever the nuns assigned you to do. At 7:00, breakfast. Get your tray and silverware, go through the line, get your oatmeal, toast, and milk. Sit down, say grace. *"Bless us, O Lord, and these Thy gifts which we are about to receive from Thy bounty, through Christ Our Lord, Amen."* Eat, no talking, no wasting time, put your tray away. Go do your little chore if yours was after breakfast. Wipe the tables off, wash the dishes. Go upstairs, go to the bathroom, get your books and homework. 7:30, go to school.

Everybody had to walk a little more than a mile to get to St. John's parochial school on the edge of downtown El Dorado. It was right next to St. John's Catholic Church, the spiritual hub of Catholic activity in town where everything happened: baptisms, confirmations, confessions, funerals. Of course, everybody had to go to the service mass before entering the school—which was a really old building. You walked up the steps to get inside. The first floor was laid out like a circle with four or five classrooms. On the second floor was a big room where plays and assemblies were held.

There were about twenty children in a classroom. Nuns were their teachers. There was Sister Owen. She was real old. She taught Latin. Sister Viola was very pretty. Sister Mary Edwardine was thoughtful, nice, took a real interest in the children. There were about a dozen others, too. They taught everything—English, math, social studies, history, religion, everything. As members of the Sisters of St. Joseph, some shuttled back and forth from Wichita, but most stayed out back at the nun's rectory. They were the corps of the Catholic diocese, the people who made things happen, the ones who served and attended to the daily needs of everybody. But when it came to the children in their classrooms, they ruled with an iron habit. No talking unless spoken to, no disruptions, no silliness, no nonsense—just learn, learn, learn. All day long, they drilled it into you.

In the afternoon, the kids filtered back to the orphanage where they immediately had to go about doing more chores. The laundry had to be done, supper had to be prepared, and the bathrooms had to be cleaned. The nuns insisted on keeping the place spotless. So the children learned to clean the bathrooms, the floors, their rooms. Everything had to be immaculate, neat, tidy, crisp. The boys were especially hounded about it. "Remember, cleanliness is next to godliness," they were told.

It was the older girls, mostly, who worked in the kitchen, helping the nuns prepare meals. The tables had to be set again, wiped clean, the dishes washed afterwards. Boys and girls both worked in the downstairs laundry next to the kitchen. It was a huge room filled with washing machines, presses, ironing boards, and big canvas receptacles on wheels that moved the dirty clothes and linens from place to place. Once washed, everything was hung out to dry in the back on clotheslines. Laundry work at the orphanage was an endless job.

After supper, homework had to be done. Then there was another mass that everybody had to attend. And religious study— lots of religious study. The children spent at least a half hour every evening studying the Baltimore Catechism.

> *Lesson One: God made the world. God is the Creator of Heaven and earth, and of all things. Man is a creature composed of a body and soul, and made to the image and likeness of God. We shall know the things which we are to believe from the Catholic Church, through which God speaks to us.*

Lastly, the children took their baths, changed into their pajamas, and said their bedtime prayers. Then it was lights out.

The daily routine on the weekends varied only from the facts that there was no school on Saturday, and everybody had to go to church on Sunday. They could sleep a little later and they could play a little longer—but for two hours and two hours only—outside on the merry-go-round, on the teeter-totter, or in various games. Then there were more chores and cleaning to do. That's one way the nuns kept the children busy. "Idle hands are the devil's workshop," they said. Just about everybody worked in the laundry on the weekends, too. Another big Saturday afternoon chore was polishing the floors—and there were a lot of floors to be polished, four full stories including the basement. So all the kids, from age nine on up had to take their turn working the floor polishers. Slowly, back and forth, up and down, careful not to miss a spot, hour after hour.

There were also holidays, when everybody got time off from chores and they had fun. There were Valentine's Day, Halloween, Thanksgiving, and Christmas. But the biggest and best of all was St. Patrick's Day—the Irish holiday when nobody had to go to school, when they had a big picnic with all kinds of games, food, candy, cake, and ice cream. Members of the community would often show up to help celebrate. The El Dorado Saddle Club would bring horses for the children to ride. Local business owners would bring hot dogs and soda pop. Members of the volunteer fire department showed up with fire engines for the kids to ride in and crawl all over.

In truth, the entire El Dorado community pitched in year around to help the kids at the orphanage. The Jeanrette Morgan School of Dancing offered free ballet, ballroom, and tap dancing lessons to the children. The local department store donated clothing. The sporting goods store gave a variety of sports equipment. The owner of the El Dorado Theater let the Home kids see movies on Saturdays every now and then. Once a month during the summer, all the kids got to go to the public swimming pool and stay there all day. The El Dorado Fishing Club sponsored tournaments and taught the kids how to fish. And on and on and on.

The City of El Dorado's support had been there right from the very beginning in 1941 when civic leader Frank S. Allen contributed $30,500 (of the $225,000 total cost) in memory of his father to help build the home. Hundreds of other smaller donations helped the Catholic church cover the rest of the costs. Construction began in September, three months before Pearl Harbor, and ended on Independence Day, July 4, 1942, when the St. Joseph Home for Children, Lewis E. Allen Memorial, opened its doors for the first time. Bishop Christian D. Winkleman, leader of the Wichita diocese at the time, called it "the fulfillment of a dream"—a "home away from home" to "serve children in need and provide for their education."

The St. Joseph Home was subsequently incorporated as a Kansas charitable corporation, and a twelve-member board of directors was seated with Bishop Winkleman serving as Chairman. Other members included the two priests at St. John's Catholic Church, Frank S. Allen, and seven other leading citizens from the city of El Dorado. At first, the board set a minimum monthly charge of twenty-three dollars per child for room and board that parents and guardians were expected to pay. But later, when it became obvious that funds could not be raised in such a manner, costs were borne by private donors and the Catholic church.

In the beginning, citizens in the community were proud of the St. Joseph Home and all it was doing for the children who lived there. As one local newspaper article described it, everything there was just wonderful:

> Inside the Home are dolls, tea parties, dancing to recorded music, singing, marbles, Indian makeups, toy tractors and cars, farm implements, and so forth. Outside on a large cement- floored playground are wagons, scooters, roller skates, basketballs, swings, slippery slides, and similar equipment. Day and night the children are never left without a supervisor. They are sweet-mannered, normal, happy, and in devotion to each other, truly marvelous . . .

> What the future may hold for these children cannot be foretold. But the present is infinitely better than that of most little people unprotected from life's storms, and it is safe to say that their future will be influenced by the guidance they are receiving and ideals being established.

Chapter Thirteen

Norma Jean Albert may have only been nine years old at the time, but she worked as hard as any of the older girls in the orphanage. Like everybody else, she sometimes cleaned the floors and worked in the laundry, but her most frequent assignment was in the kitchen where she did a little bit of everything. Tons of dishes had to be washed. Big pots and pans had to be scrubbed. Everything had to be dried and put away. And it was all done by hand—actually by little hands because the nuns didn't do kitchen cleanup work. Only the children did that.

Norma Jean also brought the food out, helped prepare it, then put it away afterwards. Sometimes she'd notice that the big pitchers of milk smelled rancid, so she would tell Sister Oswald. "No! It's not bad enough to throw out," the sister would say. "Go ahead and pour it."

By and large, food at the Home was plain, bland, unseasoned, and of small proportion. Everybody received three square meals a day but never any in-between snacks. During the week, there were usually hot dishes for supper. But on Sundays, everybody had to eat cold deviled ham sandwiches because the nuns didn't want to cook.

Many of the children were hungry all the time, including Norma Jean. But unlike the others, she would risk severe punishment by venturing into the big walk-in freezers as often as she could to sneak small bits of food out in her pockets. And once in a while, she'd go over to one of the big gallon tubs of ice cream, remove the lid, scrape off ice cream with her finger, and eat it. The children didn't get a lot of ice cream. That was for the priest and nuns.

Mostly, though, Norma Jean was lonely—very lonely.

On the weekends, she'd often sit in her room by the window that looked out over the main entrance to the Home. There she'd wait for hours on end just hoping and praying for her family to come visit. And, at first, they came fairly regularly. Her mother and grandparents visited once a month. They'd sit and talk, play some games with all the children. Clara would bounce Donald on her knee.

Her visits, though, seemed to taper off to once every couple of months after she finally had to leave little Roy at the Home permanently. Somehow, she had managed to keep him with her for three or four months—always telling Officer Mary Smith that he simply wasn't well enough yet. When she'd make her monthly visit to the Home, Donald would run out to see his little brother, who'd often sleep in the backseat of the car for the entire visit.

But the day finally came when Clara had to leave Roy there. Sister Charles, hoping to make the parting a little easier, brought mother and child to a separate room where Donald was already waiting. She reasoned that Donald would be a calming influence on Roy. But it didn't work. When the nun reached for the two-year-old, he began kicking and screaming in a most violent and hysterical manner. So Sister Charles just dragged him away and told Clara that it would be best if she'd go immediately. At that moment, all Clara could do was turn around and leave. Donald noticed tears streaming down his mother's face as she walked out.

Joe Albert visited his children once every six weeks or so. And he always brought with him a couple of grocery sacks filled with candy and cookies. Just as soon as he left, the kids would dash up to their bedrooms, empty everything out on one of the beds, and divide up all the goodies. Each time their father visited, it was like Christmas.

But both parents never visited at the same time. Joe and Clara had divorced just a few months after all the children were taken away the last time. While she remained on the farm with her parents and brothers, he lived in a small apartment in town.

Almost immediately upon arrival at the orphanage, all the Albert children started experiencing trouble in their new environment. First, four of them were held back a year in school.

Gene, Darlene, Norma Jean, and Ray were told that they weren't smart enough to be in the grade they were in—so they'd have to take it over again.

More than that, though, simply being in school was difficult. The nuns were harsh taskmasters, and often employed corporeal punishment as a means of maintaining discipline. Rulers and yardsticks were routinely used to slap students across the hands and arms. For talking in class, one boy was told to stand up and hold his hands out so the sister could hit them with the yardstick. As the nun brought the stick down, the boy pulled back his hands at the last second and the sister swung with such force that she actually broke through her habit and cut her leg.

One morning, Ray was quietly sitting in class when Sister Flora came up to him, grabbed his ear and twisted it clear around. Feeling something "pop," he reached his hand up to his ear and screamed.

"OUCH! Why did you do that?"

"I didn't like the look on your face," she responded.

For the next few weeks, Ray continually complained about his ear hurting. The nuns told him that it was nothing to worry about, that all he had was "swim ear."

"But we don't have a swimming pool," he said. "And it's winter so I haven't done any swimming at all." A couple of months later, Ray was finally sent to Dr. Johnson in El Dorado, who told him that he had a slight hearing problem in that ear. "You probably always had it, but just now noticed it," said the doctor. "Nothing can be done."

Over the years, the younger boys also had problems. Donald was awakened by two nuns in the middle of the night and taken into the bathroom. "You shouldn't sleep that way, with your hands down there between your legs," said Sister Alban. "You were playing with yourself." Only seven years old at the time, Donald didn't know what they were talking about. But the fear of God had been put into him, and from then on, he always tried to sleep with his hands on his chest.

Roy, at about the age of six, woke up one morning and went to mass as usual. He sat in the chapel with the other kids while the rosary was being spoken out loud. *"Hail, Mary, full of grace! The*

Lord is with thee: blessed art thou amongst women, and blessed is the fruit of thy womb, Jesus. Holy Mary, Mother of God, pray for us sinners, now and at the hour of our death. Amen." A child next to Roy said something that started him giggling. Suddenly a nun grabbed the four-year-old by the scruff of the neck and pulled him into one of the small rooms next to the chapel. There, she made him strip off all his clothes and then beat him with a rubber hose all over his body. He had bruises on his head, his back, and his legs that lasted for weeks. After the beating, she locked him up in the dark for an hour—just enough time to miss breakfast.

All the Albert boys were beaten by the nuns at one time or another, and usually they had to strip naked. But those small rooms, as a form of punishment, were particularly feared by the younger children. The penalty for any little misbehavior was usually either a beating or being locked up for hours in the dark. Most of the kids preferred the beatings to the pitch black isolation.

Within a few months of arriving at the orphanage, one of the twins, Gene, began to wet the bed. He had never before had this problem. But Sister Joachim was not very understanding. She really got upset about having to replace the soiled sheets morning after morning. At first, she punished him as she did all the other children who wet the bed—she wrapped the soiled sheet around his head and made him sit on the wet mattress for about twenty minutes. When the problem worsened, she embarrassed the boy by making him wear a diaper at night. But seeing no improvement after a few weeks, the nun opted for a new tactic.

One afternoon following church, she grabbed Gene by the arm and hauled him into one of those little rooms. Already waiting there was a priest. Sister Joachim proceeded to pull down the boy's pants and underwear and made him bend over a chair. Then she reached for a handful of the palm branches that had been used for the Palm Sunday mass earlier that morning. "We're going to beat that bedwetting problem out of you," said the nun as she commenced to whip Gene on his bare bottom.

As the boy began to cry, the priest started laughing. "Look at that!" he chuckled. "Look at his balls bouncing back and forth! Ha, Ha, Ha."

That first Christmas was the toughest for the Albert children. Most of them remembered last year's Christmas in Goddard when they were all reunited. There were lots of presents and lots of good food. Best of all, though, they were with their mother and father.

At the orphanage, things became a bit more cheery than usual. Everything was decorated with greenery and lights, there was a big Christmas tree down in the assembly room, and all the nuns acted a little more kindly. On Christmas morning everybody got one small present, maybe two, depending on the generosity of the local townspeople. And Joe and Clara even visited and brought each of the kids a little something.

But it wasn't the same. Mostly, the Christmas season was like the rest of the year—lonely and sad.

Right after New Year's Day, all the decorations came down and were packed in boxes. Darlene was asked by one of the nuns to help carry some of the boxes upstairs to a room on the top floor. The children were normally not allowed to be up in that area, which was essentially a huge attic used for storage.

After following the nun back to the area where the Christmas decorations were kept, Darlene set her box down and then noticed about a dozen or so larger boxes without tops. Inside each box were toys, all kinds of toys. Stuffed animals, games, balls. Dozens and dozens of toys.

Darlene couldn't believe her eyes. She knew that there was almost nothing downstairs for the children to play with. And here in this attic were all these wonderful things, but no one was allowed to play with them; no one was even allowed up there.

"Why?" she wondered. "Why?"

On the way back down to her room, Darlene ran into her big brother and told him what she had just seen in the attic. Ray immediately went to see Sister Charles.

"Please, Sister, please," begged the boy. "Let me go out and get a job so I can buy a house for all my brothers and sisters to live in."

Chapter Fourteen

One night in the late summer of 1952, Ray had just settled into bed when an older boy named Roger came over and whispered in his ear.

"Sister Agnesina wants to see you in about an hour," he said.

"Well, I might fall asleep."

"Don't worry, I'll wake you. I'm going, too."

Ray wasn't sure what to make of all this. He was only twelve years old and in the fifth grade. Roger was fourteen or fifteen. And when a sister said she wanted to see you, you went to see her. That's all there was to it. But he barely knew Sister Agnesina. A relatively young nun who had been at the Home for only a few weeks, she was on temporary assignment working with the small boys. Why did she want to see him? And why so late at night? Thinking that he had done something wrong, Ray lay awake in bed and worried until Roger came over and got him.

Moving quietly, the two boys tiptoed down the hall and made their way to Sister Agnesina's room—a very small space with only a single bed, a nightstand, a chair off to the side, and a cross on one wall. When they walked in, Sister Agnesina was sitting in the chair and another nun, Sister Harrold, was lying on the bed. Both women were out of their habits and dressed only in nightgowns. It was the first time Ray had ever seen a nun out of her habit—and he was shocked. All he could do was stand there and stare at them with wide eyes and open mouth.

Sister Harrold, he noticed, had very short hair and wasn't particularly good-looking. Sister Agnesina, on the other hand, had beautiful dark hair down to her shoulders. Not very tall, she was actually quite a beautiful woman and very well endowed.

Roger immediately got on the bed with Sister Harrold and the two started hugging and kissing. Sister Agnesina spread out a couple of blankets on the floor and laid down between them.

"Come here, Ray," she said, gracefully holding out her hand.

Ray got between the blankets with her and they started doing the same thing that Roger and Sister Harold were doing— mostly smooching. After awhile, the two started whispering to each other.

"Is it okay to do this?" asked Ray.

"Of course it is," said Sister Agnesina. "When I was at St. Mary's convent in Wichita training to be a nun, the boys used to climb over the fence and meet us in a little shed out back. Everybody does it."

"Well, how old are you?"

"I'm nineteen," she responded. "I haven't taken my vows yet."

"What was your name before you became a nun?"

"Metzinger," she said.

Ray wondered how he was going to remember that name. It was difficult to say for him so he made up a little rhyme: "Men Singing." That's how he would remember it. "Men Singing. Metzinger."

After about an hour of necking with the sisters, the boys slipped quietly back to their dormitory rooms and went to sleep.

A couple of days later, Roger told Ray that Sister Agnesina wanted to see him again. So around 11:30 that night, after everyone was in bed and fast asleep, the two boys went to her room.

As before, both women were in their nightgowns, Sister Harrold and Roger started necking on the bed, and Ray and Sister Agnesina crawled between the blankets on the floor. But then, after only ten or fifteen minutes, Roger and Sister Harold left.

"Wow, this is strange," thought Ray. "Guess I'll be leaving next."

But Sister Agnesina removed her nightgown and told him to take off his pajamas and get in bed with her. And the next thing you knew, both were in her bed, under the covers, and naked.

Necking and fondling progressed until the two became intimate. Finally, they fell asleep in each other's arms.

The next morning, Ray woke up, glanced at the clock, and saw that it was already 7:30. In the summers, that's the time all the boys got up. And Sister Agnesina had missed her morning prayers by more than an hour.

Scared to death, Ray began putting his pajamas back on.

"We overslept," he said to her. "What are we going to do?"

Sister Agnesina tried to reassure him. "Don't worry about it," she said. "I will take care of it."

"But didn't you miss your morning prayers?"

"I'll tell them I was sick."

As Ray left the room and walked out of the nun's area, he passed the smaller boys' dorm room and saw a young lad named Philip sitting up in bed looking directly at him. Trying to ignore the boy, he dashed into the bathroom for a few minutes.

When Ray finally walked into his room, Sister Richard stopped him.

"Where have you been?" she demanded to know.

"I've been in the bathroom."

"Oh, no you haven't."

"Oh, yes I have."

"Don't you lie to me, young man! I'll get to the bottom of this, one way or the other."

All morning and afternoon, Ray was beside himself wondering what was going to happen. But nobody said anything to him until Roger came up and told him that Sister Harrold and Sister Agnesina were being transferred out of the orphanage immediately.

"Well, how did they find out about it?" asked Ray.

"One of the small boys went and told."

"Where are they going?"

"Don't know."

But he later heard that Sister Agnesina had been transferred to St. Mary's of the Plains Home for the Aged in Dodge City, Kansas.

For days afterward, Ray walked around in fear just waiting for the hammer to drop. But no one ever talked to him about the incident nor even mentioned it. Several weeks later, however, Sister Richard, who was in charge of the older boys, was made mother superior of the Home. Ray always figured that she raised such a fuss over the entire episode that she forced a change in leadership.

The day after Sister Richard was promoted, Sister Owen approached Ray while he was performing his regular job cleaning the chapel. "Sister Richard wants to change your job and move you downstairs to take care of her office and the restroom down there," said the nun.

"But I kind of like my job in the chapel."

"Well, Raymond, she wants you down there. It's kind of a promotion for you," Sister Owen told him.

All kinds of things raced through Ray's mind. He figured that the reason Sister Richard insisted on the change was so that she could keep an eye on him. After all, according to the Catholic church, he had done something terribly wrong. He also thought he was probably going to Hell. And the nuns would now always look at him as a bad boy—one never to be trusted again.

Later that night, as he pulled the covers back on his bed, Ray found three holy cards resting on his pillow. He picked one up and read the words on back:

O my God! I am heartily sorry for having offended Thee, and I detest all my sins, because I dread the loss of Heaven and the pains of Hell, but most of all because they offend Thee, my God, Who art all-good and deserving of all my love. I firmly resolve, with the help of Thy grace, to confess my sins, to do penance, and to amend my life.

Chapter Fifteen

Because St. John's parochial school didn't teach grades nine through twelve, children at the orphanage were placed in foster care after completing the eighth grade. But young Ray Albert didn't want to wait that long. In 1954, he made an emotional pitch to leave after the seventh grade—continually pleading with his basketball coach, who had become something of a second father to him, to take him in. Ray just had to get out of the Home, he said. It was killing him.

After finally agreeing to become the fourteen-year-old's foster parent, Ray's coach went to authorities in the diocese and told them what he wanted to do. Sister Richard immediately agreed to the arrangement and went to work to make it happen. She secured the support of the Home's current chaplain, Father Thomas Lynch, and then worked with the coach to arrange proper approval.

So after finishing the seventh grade, Ray, at long last, was able to leave the orphanage for good. He had been in there nearly four full years—and each year had been like an eternity to him. When he finally walked out, it was a great relief—as though he had been let out of prison. Saying goodbye to his brothers and sisters, however, was one of the hardest things he ever had to do. They were still stuck in there. God, he thought, if he could only get a job and get them all out and back together. But Ray's new foster father told him to forget that idea. He was just too young to make it happen. He would have to settle for his own freedom and only periodic visits to see the rest of his family.

But the other Albert children would miss their big brother desperately. Ray had been their authority figure, their father and mother, their rock. With him gone, they all felt a huge loss—especially Darlene, who had come to rely on him even more than the others.

Perhaps subconsciously looking for a new male figure to fill the void, Darlene began to take notice of a young Irish priest who was just getting established at St. John's Parish in downtown El Dorado. Father Daniel B. Mulvihill was one of five priests to emigrate to Wichita from Ireland in 1953—and one of a dozen to arrive since 1950. He hailed from County Kerry in the southwest, had relatives in Kansas, and was a favorite of Bishop Mark Carroll, who personally ordained him at the Wichita Cathedral on February 29, 1953. Of all the Irish priests who came to the Wichita diocese in the decade of the 1950s, Mulvihill was the only one to be ordained by Bishop Carroll. All the others received their ordinations in Ireland.

Daniel Mulvihill was just the sort of man that a young girl would be attracted to. Twenty-seven years old, tall and slender with brown hair and deep-set brown eyes, he had a charming personality and a gorgeous Irish-accented tenor voice that just knocked you out. Darlene Albert, like many of the other girls her age, had a huge crush on this handsome priest who taught religion and helped coach the basketball team at St. John's school. Every day, she and her girlfriends would sit on the front row and ogle at Father Mulvihill. Then they would speak to him after class or before class—or any time the opportunity presented itself. Donald once asked Darlene why all the girls giggled whenever he came around. "Oh, you're too young," she responded. "You wouldn't understand."

Father Mulvihill liked Darlene, too. And over the years, he also seemed to take a special interest in the Albert brothers— even singling them out to take on a special fishing trip one summer's day in 1956. Gene, Dean, Donald, and Roy were very excited when one of the sisters informed them that Father Mulvihill would be coming by to take them, just them, fishing up to El Dorado Lake. They all left very early in the morning and traveled in the priest's car ten miles north to the lake. Mulvihill, who had brought extra rods, reels, and bait, patiently showed each boy how to cast their lines into the water. After only a few hours, however, the weather turned bad and they had to return to El Dorado. Just a few fish were hooked, but it was a lot of fun and an unforgettable outing for the boys.

As Father Mulvihill spent more and more time with Darlene, he began to realize that there was something special about this young girl. She had a lovely and delightful personality—always smiling, always exuberant, always vivacious. Physically, Darlene developed earlier than the other girls—filling out amply and growing into a tall, slender, beautiful young woman.

By the time 1956 rolled around, Mulvihill couldn't help but be attracted to the fourteen-year-old. So he began spending more time with her. There were a few private sessions of after-class help, a special project here or there, little notes to each other once in a while. Finally, Mulvihill approached Darlene one day and said that he was looking for a young girl to clean his residence at the parish rectory. If she was interested in the job, he could arrange for her to stay after school a couple of times a week. "It would really be helping me out, Darlene," Mulvihill told her. "What do you say?"

My God, Darlene thought to herself, that would be a dream job. Won't the other girls be jealous.

"Of course, I'll do it, Father," she quickly responded. "Anything for you. When do I start?"

Chapter Sixteen

Donald Albert spent seven years of his young life at the orphanage—from age four to eleven. And, for him, every day was a nightmare.

Get up. Have the nuns tell you what to do. Go to school. Have the nuns tell you what to do. Go back to the Home. Have the nuns tell you what to do. He hated every minute he was in their presence.

The highlight of his day was the twenty-minute walk to and from school. It was an escape—and he made the most of it. He enjoyed walking through the neighborhoods, throwing rocks up at the birds on the telephone wires, kicking cans along the streets. Often he'd walk into the neighborhood grocery store. Sometimes he had a penny or two and was able to get a couple of pieces of candy.

It was nothing less than freedom. Freedom.

At the school, the kids who had parents would park their bikes out front while they were at the service mass. Donald didn't have a bike. Neither did any of the other children at the orphanage. So he would borrow one and ride around for five or ten minutes. The wind blowing through his hair, the smile on his face. He felt at ease. He felt happy. And for those few short minutes, he felt normal. He'd always put the bike back before mass let out. They never knew—and he never hurt the bike.

When school started, it was more of the same. He lived in fear of the nuns. Whenever they said something, you had to jump.

"You're just an orphan," Sister Hillarian would tell him. "Nobody wants you. You'd better get it together, young man."

There was very little encouragement and absolutely no love or affection. You *did* walk the line—or you were severely disciplined and punished. It was like being in prison. And Donald couldn't wait for school to let out so he could walk back to the orphanage, so he could have another half hour of freedom. That walk was the highlight of his existence.

As the years slipped by, each week blended into the next. And Donald just tried to survive—any way he could. Some called him the "ornery Albert kid." He was spunky, mischievous, rebellious of the nuns' and priests' authority over him. The sisters had a lounge area where they'd go to rest, talk, and watch a little television. He knew they had a candy bowl in there. So he'd sneak around the hallway, go in and steal some—just a piece or two so they wouldn't notice. It was a game, a way to get back at them. Donald also knew where the chaplain's stash of food was kept in the big walk-in cooler. So he'd sneak in there and drink the priest's soda pop. When the shortages were discovered, the chaplain and nuns held "a Senate hearing" and, in the end, accused Dean Albert of stealing the drinks. It would be another forty years before Donald 'fessed up to his brother that he had committed the "crime."

Ever the instigator, Donald would also lead other kids into mischief. They'd climb up the drainpipes on the outside of the orphanage—all the way to the second and third floors. Sometimes they'd take the pigeons out of their nests, tie strings around their necks and make pets out of them. Some of the birds would break loose and fly away. Some ended up dead. The nuns didn't like that at all. But Donald was glad to make them angry.

Mostly, though, Donald wanted to be like other kids who weren't in the orphanage, those who lived with their parents, who had homes of their own. He wanted to be able to go into the Peter Pan Ice Cream Parlor and get a chocolate cone like everybody else. But he never had enough money. One time, Gene and Dean told him that when they went in there to deliver a newspaper, the owner gave them both a free ice cream cone. And Donald figured, "I guess I can do that, too." So the next day, he walked in, sat down at the counter and ordered a chocolate ice cream cone. When it was handed to him, he didn't even attempt to pay for it. He just jumped off the stool, ran out the door, and kept on running.

Another time, he noticed that a kid at school had a neat, brand new water pistol—and he wanted one, too. So on the way back to the orphanage that day, Donald stopped in at McClellan's Five and Dime and wandered over to the toy department. He picked a water gun off the shelf, stuck it in his pocket, and then, making certain to avoid the sales clerks, made his way out the front door. Donald also once stole a yo-yo in the same manner. No one ever caught him. Actually, no one ever even noticed. He was good at it.

Then there were the times he'd "break out" of the orphan-age on the weekends. While all the other kids were outside play-ing, Donald would sneak away and make his way along the railroad tracks and down the back alleys toward town. There were a lot of bums and hobos along that route, but Donald wasn't afraid. In fact, many of them waved and said hello to him as he walked along. And over the years, he even made a friend or two.

Once, when he arrived downtown, he walked into one of the mom-and-pop general stores. "Anybody here?" he called out. When no one answered, Donald grabbed a big bag of candy and stuffed it down his pants. Then a lady came out from the back of the store.

"How can I help you?" she asked.

"What can I get for a penny?" inquired the boy.

The lady gave him three pieces of bubble gum and took his penny. Donald then left and ate the entire bag of candy by him-self before he returned to the Home.

Another time, a young female sales clerk saw him grab a pack of baseball cards and put it in his back pocket. "Wait a min-ute," she yelled as he headed out the door. "Come back here!" Donald took off down one of the back alleys with the clerk in hot pursuit. But when he got near the railroad yard, she stopped fol-lowing him on account of the bums and hobos.

Donald also acted up at the orphanage a time or two. At the age of seven or eight, for instance, he was playing with some matches in the dormitory when the flames got out of hand. One of the wooden lockers where the kids kept their clothes caught on fire. Even though Donald quickly put it out, a pretty good burn spot was left behind.

Later that day, one of the nuns noticed the burned locker and that night there was a big shakedown. All the children had to go into Sister Alban's room, single file, one at a time, to be grilled.

"Did you start that fire?" Sister Alban asked Donald when it was his turn.

"No," he said to her with a straight face.

Then the sisters called all the kids together and said that nobody had admitted it and that if someone would just come forward and clear everything up, they wouldn't get punished for it. "Nothing's going to happen to you," said Sister Alban. "We just need to know who was playing with the matches."

Starting to feel the pressure, Donald ran outside and hid in the back barn. He waited out there in the dark until all the sisters started searching for him with flashlights. Then he sneaked back in and confessed to the chaplain.

"Now, you can't be doing things like that," said the priest. "And you can't be taking off and hiding, either."

He didn't beat Donald that night. But the nuns sure did.

Every now and then, when he was all by himself at the Home, Donald would wander up to the porch on the third floor and just stand there for hours looking off in the distance. He'd see the trains coming and going—always taking note of the black smoke puffing out of the engine's smokestack. But mostly he'd look past the railroad tracks, toward the other end of downtown, and along the street he knew his dad always took when he came to visit.

Even though he knew his dad only showed up on Sundays, Donald would still look for him every day of the week.

And he'd hope.

Hope to God that his dad would come and take him out of that hellhole.

Chapter Seventeen

Miss Joan Buchman made the forty-five-minute drive from Wichita to El Dorado once, sometimes twice a month. And if someone spotted her car coming down the road, word would get around the orphanage quick enough for a half dozen boys to gather at the front entrance to open the door for her. Blonde, five-feet six-inches tall, very attractive, and professionally dressed, Miss Buchman always had a smile and a wink for her young admirers as she strolled to the main office to speak with either the chaplain or the mother superior.

As a case worker for Catholic Social Services armed with a degree in psychology, she would select a few of the children, take them back to Wichita with her, and then run a series of tests to evaluate their mental health. She also made recommendations as to when and where they would be placed in foster care.

Miss Buchman was very familiar with the seven Albert kids, and as they grew older, she became increasingly concerned about their welfare and well-being. On numerous occasions, she attempted to set up meetings with Joe and Clara Albert to discuss the status of their children. But while Clara would show up with her parents, Joe invariably would be absent. Miss Buchman believed that Joe just did not want to answer questions about why he was claiming the children as deductions on his tax returns, but was not paying the fifteen dollars per month per child ordered by the judge.

Of more concern to her, though, was that she felt almost all of the children were not doing well at the St. Joseph Home. Some, she believed, were experiencing severe psychological problems. Others were simply withdrawn or sullen. Accordingly, Miss

Buchman decided it was best to take each out of the orphanage and place them in separate foster homes. But she needed the permission of the Sedgwick County Court, which still had official jurisdiction over the children. So on June 4, 1955, she made "oral application to the Juvenile Court for a disposition in this case"—which would grant "permanent custody and guardianship to the Catholic Social Service, Inc., on the minor Albert children," and place them in separate homes.

However, Mr. Louis J. Antonelli, a senior social worker with the Catholic Social Service, did not think that placing the Alberts in separate foster homes was such a good idea. And, on July 20, when a hearing was held on the matter, he raised enough objections that the judge in the case delayed the matter until September 7. That gave Antonelli sufficient time to put together an alternative proposal.

Louis J. Antonelli had come to Wichita in 1952 with a master's degree from St. Louis University. He was the first social worker the local Catholic Social Service ever had, and he spent thirty-seven years there, eventually retiring in 1989. During his first few years, he was the athletic coach at the orphanage, and he could see some problems, especially with the nuns. He noticed, for instance, that many of them were too heavy-handed with the children. Some beat the kids too frequently. Others had them up at 3:00 in the morning cleaning the floors, because the kids had not done a good job cleaning during the day. And then there were the nuns who had a major hang-up with the kids seeing their own naked bodies.

Antonelli learned about this particular obsession when he proposed having a shower room installed next to the gymnasium in the Home. Several of the nuns came to him and "had a flying fit" because the kids were going to see themselves and others naked. These particular nuns, he learned, were part of a religious order that required them to bathe with smocks on. They weren't even allowed to look at their own bodies so as not to be tempted sexually. This particular inhibition was transferred to the Home children in a number of different ways—including the odd demand that the kids keep their heads above a certain spot while dressing at their lockers. They were not allowed to look down and view their private parts.

After being around this sort of behavior for awhile, Mr. Antonelli began working to modify the nuns' treatment of the children. He teamed up with the crusading Sister Richard, who had been promoted to mother superior of the Home after the incident with Ray Albert and Sister Agnesina. From her, he learned that if, in early training at the convent, young nuns were troubled or had caused problems, they were sent to the orphanage rather than being given a "normal" assignment. That practice was a recipe for disaster that Sister Richard eventually was able to stop.

By the time Miss Joan Buchman filed for disposition of the Albert children, then, Mr. Antonelli had good reason to believe that any serious problems at the Home had been solved. Besides, he had gotten to know the Albert kids well and didn't think they should be separated for five or six years until they got out of high school. Rather, he thought it best to try to keep them together where they could see each other every day—so they could, at least, have *that* family contact.

On July 28, 1955, eight days after Miss Buchman's request, Mr. Antonelli filed his own petition on behalf of Catholic Social Service. He not only proposed keeping the children together but also requested full and absolute control so that they would never have to go back through the county court system. His argument was thorough, and he left nothing to chance. But in order to make it happen, he had to discredit Joe and Clara Albert.

"Said parents have been living apart since 1949," Antonelli wrote in the petition.

> Said mother has not contributed to the support of the children in over two years. Said father has not given the said children proper parental care or guardianship . . . cannot assume the obligations of a father towards the said children . . . has idle habits and . . . has been living in a house with vicious or disreputable persons.

The petition also stated that "during the past several years, the above named children have been cared for by Catholic Social Service, Inc. and petitioner alleges and states that the care, custody and control of the above named children should be given over to and vested in that agency."

Appearing in support of the petition at the September 7, 1955, hearing were Antonelli, Father Smith (the director of the Catholic Social Service), three hired attorneys, and Miss Joan Buchman, who was forced to abandon her previous position because of her boss's opposition. Then, in the presence of all, including Joe, Clara, and her parents, presiding Judge James V. Riddel Jr. (coauthor of the new Kansas Juvenile Code and former board member of the Wichita Children's Home) dismissed Miss Buchman's request "with good cause," and issued the following determination:

> It is therefore by the court considered, ordered and adjudged that said children be given over unto the care, custody and control of Catholic Services, Inc. . . . with full power and full authority to place said children in a suitable home and to consent to the adoption of any of the said children.

None of the seven Albert children were present in court, nor were they even aware of the proceedings.

Chapter Eighteen

"Raymond, come over here for a minute, will you, son?" asked Butler County Sheriff Dallas Babcock, with whom Ray was now living.

"Yes, sir?" responded the seventeen-year-old.

"I've got a letter here from the Catholic Social Services in Wichita saying that they want to send you to a boy's home in Missouri. Know anything about it?"

"What?! No, I don't know anything about it. Why would they want to do that?"

"Well, let me read this to you," said the Sheriff, who then began to read from the formal petition he'd just received in the mail. "Says here: 'Raymond Albert, for the past several months has been placed in a foster home at Towanda, Kansas, but that his adjustment to this home and the environment has not been a satisfactory adjustment.' That's not true, is it, son? You didn't complain, did you?"

"No, sir. I like it living with you and Mrs. Babcock very much. I didn't complain. I would never complain."

"Okay," said the Sheriff as he continued to read. "'Raymond Albert has been properly examined by the psychiatric consultant for petitioner and the said psychiatrist, C. J. Kurth, has recommended psychiatric treatment with the view that if the said child's condition did not improve, he might require hospitalization.' Did this doctor examine you? This C. J. Kurth?"

"No, sir. Never heard of him. Never had any examination."

"Jesus Christ! What in hell's wrong with these people?" exclaimed the Sheriff, who then continued to read.

"'The Ozanam Home for Boys at Martin City, Missouri, is a proper home within which to place the said Raymond Albert in order that he may continue his schooling and also receive proper medical care and treatment so that he may make proper adjustment and eventually become physically and mentally sound. It would be in the best interests of all concerned.'

"Well, that's what the petition dated August 29, 1956, says. Then there's this court order of the thirty-first, two days later, that grants the request."

"Oh, my God!" said Ray frantically.

"Yeah. It says: 'Petition granted to remove Raymond Albert from the State of Kansas to the Ozanam Home for Boys at Martin City, Missouri. It is so ordered.' It's signed by Judge James V. Riddel. By the way, the original petition was made out by someone named Joan Buchman. Know her?"

"Yes, I know her," responded Ray. "She's a social worker for the Catholic church. But I haven't seen her in years."

"Well, what do you think about all this? Do you want to stay here in Towanda?"

"Yes, sir. I want to stay here."

"Well, then, I guess we'll just have to fight this."

Ray had been in Towanda, Kansas, for a little over three years and was in his third foster home. He'd spent two years with his basketball coach, but just never really felt like he fit in there. Besides, he knew that the coach and his wife didn't have very much money, and his living with them was a financial strain. So when an offer from Billy Paul, one of his buddies, came along, he jumped on it. Billy's parents let Ray sleep out back in the extra bedroom over the garage. After only a few months, however, Ray was again having a difficult time. He just didn't feel comfortable there either, even though everybody was fairly nice to him.

Actually, the only place he really did feel good was working his job at the local grocery store—which was owned by Sheriff Babcock and his wife, Marie. When Ray told them about his situation, they generously offered to be his foster parents. And finally, after a few weeks of pushing papers, the church approved of the arrangement.

Ray got along great with the Babcocks from the very start. He was also doing quite well in school, where he not only had good grades but was elected president of the junior class. For the first time since he was ten years old, Ray Albert was happy— really happy.

But now, just three months after he had moved in, and one year after he had been declared a ward of the Catholic church, Sheriff Babcock received this court directive ordering the move to a boys' home in Missouri. Why were they trying to transfer him out? Ray wondered. Why now, after everything seemed to be going so well? Did somebody complain about him? It obviously wasn't the Sheriff. He seemed to be in full support. Maybe it was Miss Buchman, then. Maybe she was trying to get some government money for the church. Could that be it? Yes, that must be it, thought Ray. The church was going to get government money if he was in a State home—money they wouldn't get if he stayed with the Babcocks. Well, they wouldn't get away with it this time. He had already been in one boys' home—one where there was a convicted murderer—and he wasn't going to go to another one. He'd run away if he had to. He'd hide in a place where they'd never, ever find him.

But Ray's anxious fears were calmed after he realized what a powerful ally he had in Sheriff Dallas Babcock, who quickly retained a lawyer and set up a court date on the matter. On September 8, only one week after Ray was ordered to Missouri, he was standing in Judge Riddel's Wichita court accompanied by his foster father, the Sheriff, their lawyer, and the principal of Towanda High School—all three of whom spoke in his behalf.

At first, Ray was sent out in the hall to wait. After about twenty minutes, though, Judge Riddel called him into the courtroom. "I want to ask you a few questions, son," said the Judge.

"Yes, sir?"

"Are you going to church?"

"Well, I do go every now and then." Ray responded. "But there's no Catholic church in Towanda. And I don't feel that I want to go every Sunday."

"Why do you feel that way?"

"Because sometimes I feel that I'm being pressured."

"And you don't like to be pressured, do you?"

"No, sir. I don't."

"Okay, Raymond. That's all. You can wait outside."

After another ten minutes in the hall, Sheriff Babcock, the lawyer, and Ray's principal emerged from the courtroom with big smiles on their faces.

"Raymond," said Dallas. "You are your own person."

"Really?" said Ray. "You mean I can stay in Towanda?"

"Yup."

"Congratulations, Ray," said the principal. "The Judge set aside the order sending you to Missouri."

"He also gave you what is called 'Rights Majority,'" said the attorney. "Now you can do whatever you want to do with your life. Neither the court nor the Catholic church has any jurisdiction over you. Sheriff Babcock and your principal just wouldn't let the judge do anything else."

Ray began to cry as he hugged his foster father and then his principal.

"Thank you," he said to them. "Thank you."

On the drive back to Towanda, Ray stared out the window for a good long while. Then he turned to Sheriff Babcock. "I'm going to go get a job and get all my brothers and sisters out of the orphanage," he announced. "Now that I'm my own person, I can do it, can't I?"

"Sure can. And that's an admirable goal, son," said Dallas. "But it'll be a real uphill battle with those people at the church. Why don't we concentrate on getting you graduated from high school first?"

"Okay," said Ray. "But just as soon as I graduate, I'm gonna do it."

Chapter Nineteen

On April 5, 1956, an article regarding the St. Joseph Home appeared in the local El Dorado newspaper, the *Butler* [County] *Free-Lance*:

> The orphanage may be converted into a seminary in which teen-age boys will be prepared for the priesthood. Although several hundred boys and girls have been painstakingly cared for in the orphanage during its fourteen years, only 24 children are now enrolled. The building would accommodate 100 boys.

Six months later, Father William A. Wheeler transferred to El Dorado and became Chaplain of the Home. Born in Bray, County Wicklow, Ireland, in 1910, Wheeler was ordained in Rome (1936) for the Salesian order by Italian Cardinal Marchetti-Seiveganni, a most prestigious honor. However, over the next twenty years he bounced from diocese to diocese and, in some parts of the Catholic church, became known as a "problem priest." Specific details of those two decades have been obscured by church records. It is clear, though, that Wheeler came to the Wichita Diocese on November 9, 1955, and was immediately assigned to be an assistant at All Saint's Parish in Wichita. Eight months later, on July 16, 1956, he was transferred to St. Patrick's Parsons. And only three months after that, on October 21, he moved over to run the orphanage.

Dwindling numbers of children in the St. Joseph Home were due largely to a booming post-World War II economy. Because jobs were plentiful, there were simply not as many dependent or neglected children running around on the streets as there used to be. And while the Wichita diocese did, indeed, briefly consider turning the Home into a youth seminary for teenage boys, it eventually decided against such a move. Father Wheeler, who apparently hoped that would happen, then had to be contented to deal with the twenty children left at the Home by the time he got there. Interestingly enough, the Albert children, Darlene, Gene, Dean, Donald, and Roy, accounted for five of those twenty. Norma Jean had moved into a foster home the previous year.

Many children at the orphanage immediately noticed that there was something different and, at times, odd about this particular priest. Even though most of the chaplains they were familiar with seemed more strange and less affable than those who were stationed at St. John's Parish, at least they were fairly young men in their twenties and thirties. Wheeler, however, at age forty-six, had silver gray hair and a far more domineering and authoritative manner than the others. They also saw that he wore very fine clothes, was very neat, and insisted that when he dined, the table be set just so—with immaculate china, silverware, and a fresh flower in a vase. He would also only eat by himself, either in his quarters or in the little room off the kitchen. And the children or the nuns had to serve him.

Moreover, several of the children observed that Father Wheeler was a very heavy drinker. Often he would disappear for hours at a time and return with the smell of whiskey on his breath. Then his personality would be altered. Sometimes he would be giddy and talk a lot; sometimes he'd be mean. And frequently, he would do strange things.

Several times, he went up to the children's rooms at night just before lights out and bounced up and down on the beds until the frames broke. He also wandered around in the bathrooms and stared at the children as they were washing or taking baths. As a matter of fact, Wheeler instructed Sister Margaret to leave the doors open when the small children took their baths at night. One nine-year-old girl recalled seeing the priest's reflection in the mirror on the door as he stood out in the hall and watched them bathe. Then she crouched down low in the tub so he couldn't see her.

Father Wheeler was also quick to slap the children if they misbehaved or, God forbid, talked back to him. Once, he savagely beat a six-year-old boy in front of the other children for talking back after being admonished that he was walking on the wrong side of the street. Another time, he hauled the Albert twins, Dean and Gene, into a small room, made them strip naked in front of Sister Joachim—and then took a leather strap to them. It was nothing the boys would ever forget because of the embarrassment of having to undress in front of the nun.

And older girls at the orphanage quickly learned to stay away from the new chaplain because he was always pinching their behinds or grabbing their breasts when no one else was around. Darlene and her teenage friends always ducked into the girl's bathroom whenever they saw Father Wheeler coming down the hall. And Dean once mentioned in confession that he had been necking with one of the girls in the orphanage when, to his surprise, Father Wheeler responded: "Well, tell her to come on in here!"

Over the next eight months or so, while Darlene was keeping her distance from this "old" Irish priest, the distasteful William Wheeler, she was growing ever closer to that young Irish clergyman, the charming Daniel Mulvihill. For two, three, sometimes four times a week, she would go directly to the St. John's rectory after school—ostensibly to do housecleaning. But even though her brothers really liked Father Mulvihill, they had serious doubts about what was really going on over there. The twins, Gene and Dean, delivered papers every day after school. Frequently, one or the other of them would stop by the rectory to leave their books with Darlene to take back to the orphanage. And more than once, neither she nor Mulvihill would answer the door, even though the boys knew they were inside.

"Darlene said she was going to be here," Dean said to Gene. "Father Mulvihill's car is parked out front. What could they be so involved with inside that they can't answer the doorbell?"

Chapter Twenty

Darlene Albert was on her way to becoming a beautiful young woman—and the month of May 1957 was one of the most important of her life. First, she was unanimously chosen as the May Crowning Queen of St. John's Parish—a "great privilege" offered each year to a "chosen child" who would have the honor of placing a crown of flowers on the statue of the Virgin Mary.

The Son of God was conceived and made man by the power of the Holy Ghost, in the womb of the Blessed Virgin Mary. The Blessed Virgin Mary is truly the Mother of God, because the same Divine Person who is the Son of God is also the Son of the Blessed Virgin Mary.

May Crowning Sunday was a day of pomp and celebration. Darlene got to dress up in a beautiful white dress. Pictures were taken of her alone, with her brothers, with the priests and nuns, and with all of her classmates. Then she was the center of attention at a formal ceremony at the church. This day would be one of Darlene's most precious memories, and one of her proudest.

Then, at the end of May, Darlene graduated from the eighth grade—which formally marked the end of her stay at the orphanage. In June, she would move into a foster home and, later that fall, to a new high school.

At her formal graduation ceremony, she received a diploma marked "Special" that read: "This certifies that Darlene Albert has completed the prescribed Elementary Course of Study in St. John School, El Dorado, Kansas, and is therefore entitled to receive this certificate. May 26, 1957."

On the back of the diploma, however, was typed a caveat:

A special diploma indicates that a student has completed the course of studies prescribed for Catholic Elementary Schools of the Diocese of Wichita but is not recommended for high school without further examination by the high school to which he or she applies for admission.

If that condition created a concern for Darlene, she never voiced it to any of her brothers. Rather, she seemed unusually happy that day. After all, she was finally leaving the orphanage. And, besides, Father Mulvihill had assured her that they would see each other just as often as before.

Darlene shared her graduation with four other students, including her brother, Dean. Even though she was a year older than Dean, they ended up graduating together because she had been held back a year. Dean's twin brother, Gene, also had been held back because, as the nun told him, "You were a lazy boy." So he did not graduate with them. But all that didn't matter to Darlene. It just made the day more special to have one of her brothers as part of her class. So she saved the announcement program and, over the years, would keep it in her steadily growing photo album.

That program contained some interesting insights into the school and the children who were graduating. The class colors, it read, were blue and gold. The class flower was a yellow rose. The class motto: "If we made it through, the seventh grade can too."

Favorite sayings were listed for each of the graduates:

> Darlene Albert . . . "this here."
> Pat Russell . . . "whenever."
> Charles Walter . . . "this guy."
> Sammy Hill . . . "why."
> Dean Albert . . . "in which."

And there was also a section in the program marked "Prophecies," which was typed in by Sister Hillarian, who had gone around and asked each of the students what they might like to become in the future. Their responses were telling:

1980—The day has finally arrived when we watch Patrick Russell take the oath of office as President of the United States.

1975—Great news about Little America in the Antarctic! Charles Walter has been named the chief scientist of these expeditions by Pres. Russell.

1970—Father Sam Hill leaves El Dorado as a missionary to a foreign country as an Agriculture teacher.

1967—Dean has just completed a trip around the world studying the latest techniques in pitching and has accepted a job with the Brooklyn Dodgers.

1965—Darlene just finished a special course to become Bishop Daniel Mulvihill's special housekeeper.

Chapter Twenty-One

About a month after Darlene's graduation, in the summer of 1957, there was a gathering in the assembly hall of the orphanage to have the yearly photo taken of children and staff. Father William A. Wheeler sat at the center, flanked by the children and four nuns: Sister Joachim (the new mother superior of Home); Sister Oswald, the cook; Sister Alban, in charge of the boys; and Sister Margaret, in charge of the girls.

Most notable in the resulting black-and-white photograph were the small number of people present, which, of course, indicated that the orphanage was winding down. There were only fourteen kids in all, twelve of whom stayed in the Home on a full-time basis. The two little black girls in the picture, Susan and Beverly, were there only temporarily because their own separate facility on the other side of El Dorado closed for the summer months. It had always been that way. Every summer all the black orphans would come to the Home. Only now, fewer came than ever before.

Five of the twelve full-time resident children in the photograph were Alberts: Darlene, Dean, Gene, Donald, and Roy. Darlene was grinning at Donald, who'd just tickled her to make her smile. Four of the children (two boys and two girls) were members of the Hermes family, two others were brother and sister, and one was an only child. Sitting next to Father Wheeler, with his arm interlocked and his head affectionately leaning against the priest's shoulder, was that single little boy.

Joe Kaiser had been in the Home since he was two years old—his parents having dropped him off at the Sisters of St.

Joseph convent in Wichita, never to return or be heard from again. He was a happy-go-lucky kid, eager to please, and he always seemed to have a smile on his face. Stockily built with a large, oblong-shaped head and tight, curly blonde hair, Joe was such an angelic-looking child that the nuns routinely cast him as the lead angel in each December's Christmas pageant.

But Joe also had some problems. First of all, he was slow—not mentally retarded as some of the other kids liked to call him—just slow. And Joe was all alone. He had no brothers or sisters. No relatives to visit him at the orphanage. No friends.

The reality was that nobody wanted Joe. Even when the compassionate sisters at the convent came by the orphanage to spend the day (which occurred about once a month), he would never be selected for one-on-one time. In truth, most of the nuns were frustrated by the little boy. At St. John's parochial school, he was routinely held back and disciplined for failures in his studies. One sister got so angry at his slowness that she viciously smashed his head into a wall in front of the entire class.

But little Joe Kaiser did have one friend who took an ongoing interest in him—someone who would talk to him, hug and hold him, ease his loneliness. That person was the chaplain, Father William A. Wheeler.

The two spent a great deal of time with each other. They played games together, read together, watched television together, and spent long hours alone in Father Wheeler's apartment at the back of the Home. Joe would also serve as altar boy on trips with the priest as he made his rounds to neighboring communities that did not have a Catholic parish.

Other kids at the Home noticed the unusual amount of time this boy spent with Father Wheeler. And really, they thought nothing of it. But they also noticed that Joe seemed to have some emotional problems, as well. Even at the age of nine, for instance, the boy frequently sucked his thumb. When Donald Albert once came up and pulled it out of his mouth, Joe screamed and began swinging his fists wildly. Another time, Donald was trying to chase down his younger brother, Roy, and asked Joe to give him some help. Joe quickly complied and took off in hot pursuit. But by the time he finally caught the boy, Joe had worked himself into such an emotional frenzy that he stabbed Roy in the back with a pencil.

A serious incident or two like this one set Joe Kaiser apart from the rest of the crowd. No one else ever did anything even remotely similar. The other children just did not understand why this usually smiling, curly-haired little boy would sometimes behave so violently. And they never did find out why.

Two of the children who knew Joe well were Patty and her brother Billy [names changed]. When they arrived at the Home, Joe was very kind to them—becoming a close pal to Patty and taking Billy under his wing because he was young and didn't know anybody.

It was a rough go at first for the two new children, because their father, an alcoholic, had abused them physically, and their mother had attempted suicide. To top it off, after they were removed from their home and placed in the orphanage, they were forced to live with the harsh reality that their mother had been committed to the Larned State Mental Hospital (in Larned, Kansas) where she would remain for the rest of her life.

Patty, in particular, had a difficult time adapting to her new surroundings. Like Gene Albert, she was a bed-wetter and, on several occasions, had to endure the soiled-sheet-wrapped-around-the-head routine. She was also an unruly child, frequently getting into fights, especially when she felt her brother was being abused. In one instance, she started screaming at Sister Joachim for twisting Billy's ear—whereupon Father Wheeler grabbed her and slapped her across the mouth.

Wheeler often singled Patty out to accompany him on his rounds to the communities where he performed mass. She regularly rode alone in the car with the priest to Eureka, Augusta, and the small Kansas town of Byrne, where he was copastor at a church.

Patty just did not feel comfortable being around the old Irish priest, especially on those long car trips. For one thing, he would always introduce her as "one of the orphans from the home," rather than by her name. And she got the feeling that she was there only to make him look good. For another, he would keep a bottle of whiskey under the front seat which he would pull out on the return trips to the orphanage. She knew he didn't drink on the way there because he didn't want the parishioners to smell alcohol on his breath. That simply would not do for a Catholic priest. But on the way back, he would frequently guzzle heavily from the bottle—and that meant his mood could become anything from violent to amorous. Those were the times when she was most afraid, because she never knew what was going to happen.

On one occasion, Wheeler reached over, put his arm around her, and pulled her across the front seat next to him. Holding her tight, he said: "Why don't you suck me off?"

Patty was only nine years old and really didn't know what that meant. But she was sure it was not something she wanted to do.

"No! Leave me alone!" she said as she jabbed the priest in the ribs with her elbow. Then Patty slid back across the seat and just stared out the window for the rest of the trip.

Not another word was spoken in the car that day. But a couple of nights later, Father Wheeler came into the girls' dormitory where Patty was reading by herself.

He slowly closed the door, flipped off the light switch, and turned the lock on the door—the one that the children were ordered never to touch. Then he took her by the hand, sat down on a bed, and forced her to get on her knees in front of him.

This time the little girl was scared—really scared. The priest's grip on her was powerful and it hurt her. The look on his face was menacing. She had never seen that look before. And the strong smell of whiskey was on his breath.

So Patty did not resist. She was too frightened to do so—afraid of what he might do to her.

Wheeler dropped his trousers and exposed himself. Then he grabbed the little girl and slowly pulled her toward him.

Patty has no memory of what happened after that. But she does remember going to bed afterwards—and saying her regular bedtime prayers:

Now I lay me down to sleep. I pray the Lord my soul to keep. If I should die before I wake, I pray the Lord my soul to take. God bless mama, papa, Billy, all the other children, Sister Joachim, Sister Oswald, Sister Alban, Sister Margaret, and Father Wheeler. Amen.

Chapter Twenty-Two

"Introiba ad altare dei," said Father William A. Wheeler. "I will go to the altar of God." The bells rang and everybody stood up. Then Father Wheeler walked out onto the altar from a side room and offered the opening blessing.

"This mass is in praise of the Albert boys," he said in his thick Irish accent. "May the Lord be with them so they have a safe trip. May their futures be bright. May God, in all his wisdom, protect them and care for them and love them. In the name of the Father, the Son, and the Holy Ghost. Amen."

After several scripture readings, Sister Joachim came forward to say a few words. "In a couple of days, Dean, Gene, Don, and Roy will be leaving for Boys Town in Nebraska," said the nun. "They came to our St. Joseph Home seven years ago in 1950. We have watched them grow and we are very proud of them. Today, we celebrate them. We ask all to say prayers for them so that they may have a safe trip—and so they may gracefully make their adjustments in life."

Father Wheeler then took over and administered communion to all the children. When each Albert brother came to the altar, he placed his hand on their heads and offered another special blessing of protection. Shortly thereafter, the service ended with the recitation of the Lord's Prayer:

> *Our Father, Who art in Heaven, hallowed be Thy name. Thy kingdom come. Thy will be done on earth as it is in Heaven. Give us this day our daily bread. And forgive us our trespasses, as we forgive those who trespass against us. And lead us not into temptation, but deliver us from evil. Amen.*

This mass was held in the small chapel of the orphanage on the last Sunday the four Albert brothers would ever spend there. Later that week, Father Wheeler would drive them all up to Boys Town where they would reside until they graduated from high school.

The St. Joseph Home for Children was in its last few years of operation, and for the first time, rumors of child abuse were beginning to surface around town. People were whispering about "kids being beaten by the nuns," or "priests doing some unspeakable things."

And it wasn't just in El Dorado, Kansas. Catholic orphanages were quietly being phased out and shut down all across the country—their children placed in foster homes on a regular, almost methodical basis. Overall, the thought that there would be problems in such religious-run institutions of charity never entered the minds of most people—especially those in the public domain.

Internal to the church, however, an air of secrecy and shame surrounded all the hearsay. The Catholic bishops worked hard to keep things hushed up. The Irish priests stuck together and helped cover for each other. And members of local communities were reluctant to speak openly. "We're not supposed to talk about Father," was the prevailing sentiment.

In Wichita, Louis J. Antonelli worked hard to place all the Albert children in the best places possible. After months of detective work, he had finally located some relatives who were willing to take in Darlene. In late June of 1957, she moved in with her aunt and uncle in Walnut, Kansas—about 140 miles east of Wichita. In addition, Mr. Antonelli's goal of keeping the Albert brothers together never waned. He pulled countless strings, called in favors, and lobbied tirelessly, until at last he was able to get all four of them admitted into Boys Town. It certainly wasn't easy, but he did get them in.

The morning after holding the special mass, Father Wheeler instructed the Albert boys to be in the chapel at 1:30 in the afternoon so he could give them their physicals. They had to be examined, he said, before they went to Boys Town. Gene, Donald, and Roy showed up promptly, but Dean was nowhere to be found. It turned out that he had been given permission to go on an errand with one of the nuns, but the other boys did not know it at the time.

Since Gene was the oldest, he figured he should be the one to go tell Father Wheeler that three of them were waiting. So he headed out the back of the second-floor chapel and onto the elevated walkway that led to the front door of the chaplain's apartment about one hundred feet away.

Gene knocked and heard the words, "Come in."

When he entered, Father Wheeler was sitting on the couch. "Hello, young man," he said. "Come over here. I want to check you over."

Gene then walked over and stood in front of the priest.

"Okay, now drop your pants and underwear."

After Gene did what he was told, Father Wheeler ran his hand up the inside of the boy's thigh and began fondling his private parts. This went on for four or five minutes until the priest abruptly stopped.

"Okay, that's it. You can get dressed and go."

Embarrassed and humiliated, Gene quickly pulled up his trousers and headed out the door.

"Call in the next one," Father Wheeler shouted out.

When Gene passed rapidly through the chapel, all he said was: "Your turn, Donald."

As with Gene, Wheeler performed the "physical" in much the same manner—only he asked Donald to "turn around and bend over." Then he spread the cheeks of the eleven-year-old's buttocks and "inspected" his anal area.

When it was the youngest brother's turn, Wheeler fondled the boy's genitals for a few minutes, and then took Roy's hand and placed it on his own erect penis. The nine-year-old was shocked. He had absolutely no idea what was happening, and after what seemed like an hour to the boy, the priest finally told him he could go.

A few days later, on July 2, 1957, the time finally came when the last of the Albert children were to leave the orphanage for good. Forty years later, Gene would recall every detail as if it had happened yesterday.

He remembered feeling apprehensive to finally be leaving the Home after so many years there. After all, aside from going to and from school, they had only been allowed to leave the grounds once every couple of years or so. And those times were limited to a special away basketball game, a trip to Augusta, Kansas, with Father Wheeler to help him serve mass in a farmhouse, and that memorable fishing trip with Father Mulvihill. Never once were he and his brothers allowed to visit his grandparents at the Martin family farm in Wichita. Never once. Now, all of a sudden, they were headed hundreds of miles north to a new state and a new home. It was really kind of scary for a boy his age.

They were taking the six-hour trip from El Dorado to Boys Town in Father Wheeler's old Ford station wagon. And they were going to travel to Kansas City and pass through Missouri and Iowa before arriving at their destination. So it was also going to be kind of an adventure.

That morning, all the brothers got up early, ate breakfast, finished their packing, and then waited around until it was time to go. Finally, at about 9:30, Father Wheeler loaded their suitcases into the back of the station wagon—including the one Darlene had given Roy and Donald as a going away present. That gift meant a lot to them, because their sister had spent most of the money she had to buy it.

All the nuns and children were gathered around the car as Father Wheeler instructed Dean and Gene to get in the back seat. "Donald and Roy need to be in the front seat," he said. "That way, there'll be more room."

Gene never forgot the scene as he looked out the back window while they headed down the road. The children and sisters were waving goodbye—getting smaller and smaller—the large, red brick St. Joseph Home for Children finally fading away in the background.

There wasn't much conversation in the car, because the boys were too busy looking out the windows, soaking in all the new sights. And the priest seemed to be concentrating on his driving. But several hours into the trip, Father Wheeler suddenly grabbed Donald's hand and placed it on his erect penis. The boy pulled back several times, but Wheeler kept grabbing his hand and putting it back.

After about fifteen minutes of this back-and-forth routine, they arrived at the outskirts of Kansas City and stopped at a small café for lunch. Everybody piled out of the car—Donald fastest of all. In fact, he almost crushed Roy as he pushed him out the passenger door.

Inside the restaurant, all the boys ordered hamburgers, cokes, and got a cookie for dessert. Before going outside, everybody went to the bathroom—and when they went to get back into the car, Donald waited until Roy got in the front seat first. He did not want to sit in the middle, no matter what.

As the station wagon pulled out, Donald noticed that Father Wheeler started doing the same thing to his little brother and that Roy was pulling away just like he did. But, unlike with him, the priest was also placing his hand on Roy's lap and fondling the boy's privates. Then he noticed that Wheeler took Roy's hand and placed it on his own erect penis with such a strong grip that his little brother simply could not pull his hand back. Donald just turned and stared out the window. He didn't know what else to do.

The twins in the back seat had no idea what was going on up front. But Dean did wonder what in hell Father Wheeler was talking about when he suddenly yelled out:

"Hold on tight going around the corner!"

Chapter Twenty-Three

In the summer of 1957, while the old Irish priest, Father William Wheeler, was driving the Albert boys 350 miles north of Wichita to Boys Town, the young Irish priest, Father Daniel Mulvihill, was headed 180 miles east to take a new job in Pittsburg, Kansas. He had spotted an opening for an assistant pastor at a small parish there and, as soon as he saw it, had applied and lobbied hard for the position.

Why?

Because Pittsburg was only twenty-five miles away from Walnut, Kansas, where Darlene was being placed into foster care. Not only would he be able to see her on a regular basis, but any way you cut it, a half-hour drive was better than a four-hour drive.

In Walnut, Darlene lived with her mother's older brother, John Martin, his wife, Cornelia, and their four children. The Martins were quiet, lifelong farmers. They lived a simple life, worked hard during the week farming several hundred acres, and attended church every Sunday at Our Lady of Lourdes in Pittsburg. According to official records of the Wichita Diocese, Daniel Mulvihill began his new job there on June 8, 1957—the very same week that Darlene arrived in Walnut.

As a matter of fact, it was Mulvihill who drove Darlene to the Martin farm. John and Cornelia did not think it was unusual at all to have a Catholic priest transport their niece to them. After all, she was a ward of the Catholic Charities organization, and besides, that's one of the things men of the cloth did. However, they had absolutely no idea as to the nature of the relationship between their fifteen-year-old niece and their new thirty-year-old Irish pastor. No one did.

Darlene was a fairly outgoing and talkative girl, but during the time she lived with her aunt and uncle, she never discussed Father Mulvihill. Not ever. Even when she would return to the farm after spending many a Sunday afternoon after church with him, she would not comment on what she did or how they spent their time together.

Cornelia Martin would have been glad to formally adopt her husband's niece, but Darlene herself was against it. She'd had a tough time adjusting to the new surroundings. Being out on a farm alone, going through her early, unsettling teenage years, and just the big change in general all contributed to a feeling that she simply did not fit in. In addition, Darlene struggled academically. Initially enrolled at St. Patrick's Catholic High School, she found the curriculum much tougher than she'd experienced in El Dorado, and her grades suffered as a result. In an effort to ease Darlene's distress over the failing marks, the Martins transferred her to Walnut's public high school halfway through her freshman year. But not only did her grades fail to improve, Darlene became even more upset, because she was forced to try and make new friends all over again.

By the time summer rolled around, both she and the Martins agreed that it was time for her to enter a new foster home. Unfortunately, the Catholic Charities were taken off guard by this surprise decision. They never dreamed the situation would not work out, because after all, Darlene had moved in with family.

As a stopgap measure then, Darlene was moved into a temporary foster home back in El Dorado until a permanent placement could be arranged. With some sensitivity toward her recent struggles, the social workers planned for her to stay one full academic season at El Dorado High School so that her sophomore year would not be interrupted.

The entire idea of Darlene's relocation annoyed Father Mulvihill, who was now stuck in the small town of Pittsburg. Having only been at Our Lady of Lourdes for one year, there was just no way he would be allowed to transfer back to El Dorado. Except in special situations, tours of duty for priests rarely lasted less than two years. And Mulvihill wasn't eager to request a change, because someone might start to suspect his motives.

Darlene, on the other hand, was pretty upbeat about the move, because she was familiar with her new foster parents, Bill and Marie Rex. Bill was a nice man, a prominent businessman in El Dorado. He owned a local bank, the Farm and Home Furniture store, and was a partner in Rex and Morris Oil Company. Moreover, his wife, Marie, was one of the kindest and most benevolent of the good citizens of El Dorado, who had supported the St. Joseph Home for years. On a regular basis, she would go to the orphanage and take all the girls to the beauty parlor to have their hair done. Darlene simply adored her. And so did her brothers, Dean, Gene, Don, and Roy, who would never forget Mrs. Rex driving all the way to Boys Town in November 1957 just to take them out to a fine restaurant in downtown Omaha for their first Thanksgiving dinner away from the Home.

Overall, Darlene's year with Mr. and Mrs. Rex was a positive one. Being back in El Dorado reunited her with all of her old friends. She got to live in the Rex's beautiful home out on the lake. Her grades at El Dorado High improved tremendously. And she began to develop into a more confident, outgoing, and spirited young woman.

But once again, when the school year was over, Darlene had to say goodbye to all of her friends, because the Catholic Charities had located a permanent foster home for her in Wichita. This time she would be living with the Jabars, a prosperous Lebanese family who owned a well-known grocery store called the Indian Hills Meat Market. Mr. and Mrs. Jabar had three teenage children of their own and lived in a beautiful, high-income development near the midtown riverside area of Wichita.

In September, 1959, Darlene began her junior year at Wichita High School North. Less than six months later, on February 22, 1960, Father Daniel B. Mulvihill arrived in town to assume a new position. He was to be the assistant pastor at Blessed Sacrament Catholic Church—located barely four miles from the Jabar's residence.

Chapter Twenty-Four

Early in her junior year at North High, Darlene contemplated dropping out of school and getting a job. She was weary of all the moves, apprehensive about starting over again, and her grades were only so-so. Things just weren't going well.

But as time passed, she began to meld smoothly into her new environment—both in high school and at home. The Jabars turned out to be extraordinarily kind and considerate people. She liked living with them. And pretty soon, Darlene forgot all about dropping out and began to enjoy her life. The truth was that her junior and senior years in Wichita were among the happiest of her life. She had many girlfriends with whom she spent considerable time. She enjoyed swimming, and she played a lot of tennis.

Classmates who signed Darlene's 1961 senior yearbook commented on her cheery nature, her friendly disposition, and her sweetness. To them, she was "a swell kid," "a wonderful person," and "a grand girl." "If you continue your sweetness, you're sure to be a success," wrote one. "Keep your sweet smile and you'll go places," inscribed another.

Curiously, though, Darlene stood out in her yearbook not so much for the activities in which she took part, but for those in which she did not participate. Next to class pictures of seniors were listed all kinds of extracurricular activities. For the girls, there were things such as: Red Arrows, Y-Teens, Glee Club, Choir, Spanish Club, Junior Red Cross, Future Teachers, and the Pep Club. But next to Darlene Frances Albert's picture, there were no activities mentioned—not one. In addition, while twenty-three girls signed her senior annual, only three boys did. And none of Darlene's girlfriends remember her ever going out on a date. She seemed to avoid any contact with the boys at her high school—even though many had asked her out.

Part of Darlene's nonparticipation in extracurricular activities and her general avoidance of boys was due to the fact that she was deeply involved in an intimate love affair with Father Daniel Mulvihill. They saw each other frequently. Two or three times a week, she would go over to his house after school, and just as before in El Dorado, people were told that Darlene was Father Mulvihill's special housekeeper. Sometimes, Mulvihill would drive up to the Jabars' house to pick her up for "a special event at the church" or "to go over to Blessed Sacrament for Bible study." And always, after every Sunday service, Darlene would linger around the church and then spend the afternoons with Mulvihill. He would then drop her off at the Jabars' in time for their family dinner—in which he would sometimes be invited to partake.

This cycle of activity continued on a regular basis right up until Darlene graduated from high school on May 31, 1961. Academically, she had finished in the bottom third of a class of 529 seniors. But she had graduated and was proud of it. The next week, Darlene moved in with her sister, Norma Jean, who lived at the Interdale apartment complex in the 900 block of North Broadway Street—only a few miles from the Jabars' residence and still very close to Blessed Sacrament Catholic Church.

Norma Jean had lived in Wichita since leaving the orphanage in 1956. She'd been placed in a foster home with a nice family and had attended Sacred Heart Catholic High School. During that time, the only one of her siblings she kept in constant contact with was her sister. She did not communicate with older brother Ray, even though he lived and worked only a few miles away. And she visited her younger brothers at Boys Town only one time. That visit occurred during her senior year, and they would never forget all the other boys going to the windows and pulling up the blinds to get a good look at her. Norma Jean had developed into a tall, slender, dark-haired, very good-looking young woman.

Norma Jean did, however, keep in contact with her mother and father. And in late May of 1959, Joe Albert happened to mention to his son that Norma was going to graduate from high school that coming Saturday.

"Are you going?" asked Ray.

"Nope," came the curt response.

"Well, somebody ought to go."

Even though Ray had not even seen his sister in more than three years, he made it a point to be sitting in the stands at the Sacred Heart auditorium during the graduation ceremony. He watched proudly as Norma Jean, dressed in her cap and gown, walked in with the other graduates and then received her diploma. Afterwards, he went up, said hello, and gave his sister a bear hug. Tears came to her eyes as she said thank you to her big brother for being there. She had not expected anybody to show up. But Ray wouldn't have missed it. He was happy that night—happy and proud that at least one of his siblings had survived and made it out of government- and Catholic-sponsored control.

By the time Norma invited Darlene to move in with her in June of 1961, she had already been employed for two years at St. Francis Hospital. As a secretary, she was making a decent salary, paying about $65 a month in rent, and felt able to support her sister until she could find a job of her own.

But Darlene wasn't in a hurry to find employment right away. She wanted to take a little time off, relax, and enjoy her newfound freedom. And Norma Jean didn't press her to find employment. Actually, she liked having her sister around to do things with.

For most of the summer, the two had a grand time. They went out to eat, went to movies, played tennis, and went swimming together. During one of those outings, Norma Jean snapped a picture of Darlene in her bathing suit. The resulting black-and-white photograph revealed a voluptuous young woman: five feet, nine inches tall, about 130 pounds, slender with beautiful bone and facial structure, olive complexion, dark brown hair, and brown eyes. There was no doubt about it. Darlene Albert, at the age of nineteen, was strikingly beautiful.

Also that summer, Norma Jean, touched by her brother's attendance at her graduation, made it a point to stay in regular contact with him. In mid-August, the two were having lunch together, when halfway through what was turning out to be a very amiable conversation, Ray inquired about their sister.

"How's Darlene?" he asked.

Norma Jean paused for a moment and then gazed down at her food.

"I think Darlene may be pregnant," she told Ray. "Her breasts are getting larger."

Chapter Twenty-Five

Sometime during the third week in August of 1961, Darlene told Father Mulvihill she was pregnant—almost four months pregnant—with his child.

She hadn't wanted to tell him early on, when she first became worried. Actually, she had hoped beyond hope that it wasn't true. Maybe she really wasn't going to have a baby. Maybe it was just her imagination. But now that she was beginning to show, she had no other choice. Besides, Darlene was afraid—really afraid. Not only was she pregnant out of wedlock, but the father was a Catholic priest. My God! What was she going to do? She was in trouble and needed help. She simply had to tell someone—and he was the only person she could speak to about it.

What went through Mulvihill's mind can only be imagined.

He was a thirty-four-year-old priest who had gotten a teen-age girl pregnant. For starters, he had broken his vow of celibacy:

People should cultivate [chastity] in the way that is suited to their state of life. Some profess virginity or consecrated celibacy which enables them to give themselves to God alone with an undivided heart in a remarkable manner [Baltimore Catechism].

He had also committed a very basic sin that was especially damning for a man of the cloth.

Fornication is carnal union between an unmarried man and an unmarried woman. It is gravely contrary to the dignity of persons . . . Moreover, it is a grave scandal when there is corruption of the young [Baltimore Catechism].

Worst of all, however, was the undeniable fact that he had conducted an ongoing lascivious relationship with Darlene since well before she became of legal age.

> *Rape . . . causes grave damage that can mark the victim for life. It is always an intrinsically evil act. Graver still is the rape of children committed by . . . those responsible for the education of the children entrusted to them* [Baltimore Catechism].

If all this were to get out, Mulvihill's entire career within the Catholic church would be ruined—and he would be subject to criminal prosecution.

Jesus! What was he going to do?

Rather than panicking, Mulvihill turned to the one group of people he knew would keep safe his terrible secret and help him cover it up. He turned to the fraternity of Irish Catholic priests. And who was the leader of this group in the Wichita Diocese? None other than his mentor and good friend, William A. Wheeler. So, within the week, the young Irishman drove fifty miles to Hutchison, Kansas, where Wheeler was now located.

After the St. Joseph Home for Children closed back in December of 1959, Wheeler had applied for and received a transfer there to the State Reformatory for Boys. The pedophile priest was quite happy in his new assignment, because he was able to stay around young children and remain out of the spotlight. When Mulvihill contacted him, he had been serving (since October 1960) in dual capacity as chaplain of both the reformatory and St. Elizabeth's Mental Hospital.

"Is there any way out of this?" Mulvihill asked Wheeler. "What will they do to me?"

The older priest was calm and reassuring. "It'll be all right, Daniel," he said. "This has happened before. I can take care of it. All I have to do is make a few calls. It'll take a few days."

"Good," replied the much-relieved younger priest. "What do I do in the meantime?"

"The first thing you have to do is to get the girl under control. Reassure her that there are institutions set up to help young girls like her who are in trouble—and that we're setting things up now. Tell her the Church will help her."

"Okay."

"But you'll also have to put the fear of God into her to make sure she keeps quiet. Here's what you need to tell her . . ."

Several days later, Mulvihill sat down with Darlene and had a long talk. He lectured her about the stigma associated with out-of-wedlock pregnancy. If it were to get out, the consequences would be numerous. She'd be treated horribly. She'd be shamed and shunned, her life made insufferable. Friends and family would abandon her if they found out. She'd be denounced by the church. "In short, Darlene, your life will be ruined if you don't do as I say."

Then he went over what needed to be done. First of all, he said that abortion was not an option. It was not only illegal, it would be a sin against God. Don't forget the Fifth Commandment, he told her.

Thou Shalt Not Kill.

The thing to do was to hide her from view. They must turn to an institution that catered specifically to young girls in her position—a maternity or infant home run exclusively by the Catholic church. Such places were established, in part, so abortion would never be an option. It would be a place for her to stay until she had her child. Then she would put the baby up for adoption. "We're setting all that up now."

No mention was made by Father Mulvihill of what Darlene wanted most to hear from him. He did not even consider leaving the priesthood to marry her. And that confused Darlene. She didn't understand why. If he really loved her, as he had said many times over the years, then why wouldn't he marry her? Besides, didn't the Bible say that's what he was supposed to do?

> *If a man seduces a virgin who is not betrothed, and lies with her, he shall give the marriage present for her, and make her his wife.* (Exodus 22:13)

Meanwhile, Wheeler had finally made contact with his buddy, an Irish priest in Kansas City.

"We've got a problem. One of our brothers, a grand Irishman, is in a wee bit of trouble. He's gotten a girl pregnant. He's young. Very worried. We must help him."

After arrangements were made, Wheeler got back to Mulvihill.

"Okay, here's what you do. There are four Catholic- sponsored maternity homes in Kansas City. Give the girl this phone number. It's to the St. Anthony's Infant Home at 1414 East Twenty-Seventh Street. She should call them herself. Tell her not to use her real name. She should give the name Janet Wheeler. We've told them she's my niece. They're expecting her call."

Darlene did as she was told. She called and made arrangements to check into St. Anthony's by mid-September. When the time came to leave, on September 12, 1961, Father Mulvihill drove her to Kansas City. It was just the two of them in the car, and because Darlene was still very frightened, he held her hand for most of the ride. Three hours later, he was by her side as she checked in to St. Anthony's. Father Mulvihill was her priest, they said. He was providing a guiding hand on behalf of his good friend, Father William A. Wheeler. Janet, here, is his niece.

The nuns did not question the priest's authority. Almost all of the sisters who served at the Home were older nuns—schooled in compassion for the young girls in their charge and obedient to the authority of priests. Besides, it was not unusual for a priest to accompany a pregnant, unwed teenager to the Home.

"Come now, my dear," said Sister Mathilde Comstock. "We'll show you to your room, and after you get settled, you can fill out the necessary paperwork."

Father Mulvihill gave Darlene a hug and assured her that everything would be all right. He would call her the next day to see how she was doing. Then, with a great feeling of relief, he got in his car and drove back to Wichita by himself.

About an hour later, Darlene sat down with caseworker Mary Alice McDermott to record basic information. "The mother contacted Catholic Charities in September seeking assistance in adoptive placement of her unborn child due in January 1962," she wrote. "Plans were made for her to work until January and she entered St. Anthony's on the 12th of September."

Also entered into the record were the following facts and information:

Name: Janet Wheeler. *[Fictitious name.]*

Address: 840 N. Topeka, Maize, Kansas *[No such address, but Maize was the town of Darlene's birth.]*

Education and Employment: Mother completed high school and had worked as a nurses' aide. She has some hope of becoming a practical nurse and may enter training in the fall. *[Darlene had never worked as a nurse's aide.]*

Own Background: She lost contact with her brothers and sisters with the exception of one older sister whom she sees often. *[Darlene had not lost contact with her brothers. She had only one sister.]*

Alleged Father: Mother had dated this boy about a year and they had talked of marriage. She did tell him of her pregnancy but he offered no plan nor assistance. When she realized his attitude she decided against marriage and was convinced it would never work. *[False statement.]*

Description of Father: This young man is 21 years of age and of Irish nationality extraction. He is described as 6' tall and weight is estimated at 160 lbs. He too is dark in coloring and has brown hair and brown eyes. *[Mulvihill was 34 at the time. Other than age, general description fits him.]*

Education and Employment of Father: He finished high school and the last job he had was as a clerk. *[False statement.]*

Religion and Health of Father: Alleged father was Catholic and had been baptized in infancy. His general health is excellent and mother knows of no negatives that would deter placement. *[All true.]*

Maternal Relatives: Sister is twenty-four and married. She is a high school graduate. This young woman, too, is olive in coloring with dark hair and dark eyes. *[Norma Jean was twenty-one and unmarried. Otherwise, all true.]*

Parents: She is sure her father is deceased but only presumes her mother is living. *[Darlene's father, Joe, was very much alive—as was her mother, Clara, with whom she had been in regular contact.]*

Chapter Twenty-Six

On August 24, 1961, during the very same week that Darlene revealed her pregnancy to Mulvihill, Clara Albert was taken to Larned State Mental Hospital by her parents.

Clara's mental health had been steadily going downhill for years—ever since her children had been taken away for the final time in 1950. Among other things, she had fought extended bouts of depression, sometimes not getting out of bed for weeks on end. She felt that everybody was out to get her—the government, the church, her parents, Joe. And at times, she experienced delusional events that bordered on hysteria. Most recently, she had become violent—throwing things, threatening to kill her parents, her brothers, herself, and anyone that came near her. After that particular outburst, her father and brother, Stephen, drove her straight to Larned. They could no longer handle the situation themselves. She needed help, serious medical help.

Physicians immediately put Clara on medication to control her hysteria and calm her down. Then they gave her a complete physical and mental examination. After lab test results were completed, it was revealed that she was suffering from an advanced case of syphilis. When the doctors asked her parents for some history, the Martins informed them that she could only have contracted the disease through her ex-husband, Joe Albert, and that she must have been suffering from it for at least eleven years. Clara, they said, could not possibly have had a sexual relationship with anyone else since 1950.

Institutional paperwork recorded her situation as follows:

Mrs. Albert, a 48-year-old white, divorced housewife was admitted for the first time on 8-24-61. Her mental illness became evident several years after her marriage. Both Mr. and Mrs. Albert were arrested and held in jail for neglecting and abandoning their children. Patient often had spells during which she threatened to kill her parents. Patient was found to have had syphilis and it was believed by the patient's family that this disease was contracted through her husband. Patient adjustment in the hospital was good. Her orientation was accurate and the sensorium clear but insight was absent. She was placed on medication and had O.T. assignment.

In September, Ray Albert drove out to the Martin farm on a Saturday afternoon to visit his mother.

"She's not here," his grandmother told him. "She's been in Larned for awhile now, Ray. She's real sick."

The next day, Ray drove two-and-one-half hours west to Larned, Kansas, to visit his mom, where he found her quiet, sedated, and unusually sad. Worst of all, though, he hated the institution she was in. The hallways, the rooms, the prison-like atmosphere—it all really alarmed him. So, on Monday morning, Ray took a couple of hours off work and went to see Mr. Francis Hesse, an attorney for the Catholic church who had previously handled his case.

"Mr. Hesse, are you aware that my mother is confined to the Larned Mental Hospital?" he asked.

"Yes, Raymond. I'm very familiar with the entire situation."

"Well, I want her out of there. I'm twenty-three years old now. I've got a good job. I want her to move in with me. I'll take care of her."

"Listen to me carefully, Raymond," said Mr. Hesse. "You're not capable of taking care of your mother. There is no way you could handle the situation. She is just too far gone."

Shortly thereafter, Clara Albert's case was adjudicated and she was formally committed to the Larned mental institution. "Her diagnosis was made Schizophrenic reaction," read the paperwork, "[and] paranoid or chronic brain syndrome associated with central nervous system syphilis, Meningoencephalitic type (paranoid)."

Chapter Twenty-Seven

St. Anthony's Infant Home was nestled in a peaceful woodland setting on the edge of a quiet residential neighborhood in Kansas City, Missouri. The former Fairmount Maternity Hospital, it was remodeled to reflect similar Irish institutions and rededicated on July 10, 1955, as a Catholic-run home for unwed mothers and their infants. Not only was its architecture Irish, St. Anthony's attitudes and practices toward unwed mothers reflected the values and biases of Irish Catholicism, as well.

The building was long and rectangular in shape with four levels, including a full basement level. While not quite as large, and with a facade of white brick rather than red, it was remarkably similar to the St. Joseph Home for Children, where Darlene had spent much of her childhood. As in the orphanage, the lower level housed the kitchen, cafeteria, and laundry. On the first floor were offices, meeting rooms, the chapel, and several nurseries. The upper two floors were mostly bedrooms.

Typically, there were twenty-five girls in residence at the Home and another thirty receiving assistance and counseling on an outpatient basis. It was staffed by experienced nuns who had extensive training in nursing, education, social work, and counseling. As a matter of fact, St. Anthony's was so professionally run that girls who had not yet completed high school were able to continue their studies right there. Medical care was also readily available onsite as were both psychological and social counseling.

When the time came for girls to have their babies, they were transported to the nearby St. Mary's Hospital for delivery and recovery. Almost all babies were put up for adoption through the Catholic church, which was sanctioned by the State of Missouri.

There were, however, a few cases where a girl would decide at the last minute to keep her baby, but that was more the exception than the rule. Usually the mothers signed relinquishment papers and left St. Anthony's within a month. Infants, however, were kept at the Home—sometimes until they were up to two years of age. If not adopted by then, they were sent to the nearby St. Joseph Home for Girls.

A typical day for the young mothers-to-be began when they rose at 6:00 AM and attended a 6:30 AM mass. After breakfast, they all had their jobs to do, including: cooking, washing dishes, scrubbing floors and bathrooms, general housecleaning, and working in the laundry. The girls also tended to the newborn babies who were lined up in row upon row of cribs in room after room on the second floor. They did everything one might expect—holding the infants, feeding them, dressing them, changing their diapers, and so on. They would also bring the babies to and from prospective adoptive parents who would come by to view or hold the infants. Each young woman was paid a small compensation for performing her job. But if she didn't work, she was billed for her room and board.

Because all the girls were in the same situation, they tended to befriend each other. However, these friendships were both superficial and short-lived. The girls were allowed to address each other by first names only, many of which (as in Darlene's case) were fictitious. No girl ever knew the true identity of the other girls at the Home. And after their babies were born, they'd leave St. Anthony's and return to their respective communities, never to see each other again.

Doctors who examined Darlene listed her official due date as the last week in January, 1962. That placed conception some-where around the first of May, 1961—a full month before she graduated from high school. But Darlene ended up carrying the baby for an extra week to ten days. Finally, late on the evening of February 6, she went into labor and was quickly taken to St. Mary's Hospital where she gave birth to a healthy baby boy. According to official records, her delivery was "normal" and "without complications."

She stayed in the hospital for a week and, while there, paid the company of Stickman and Moreano a small fee to put together a birth announcement. On the front of the little card was a sketch of a baby in a bassinet. Darlene named her son "Bill Patrick." He was born February 7, 1962, at 1:31 AM He weighed seven pounds, eight ounces and was twenty inches long.

Despite having a lot of people around, it must have been lonely for a young girl like Darlene. Being away from family and friends. Having those feelings of isolation, abandonment, wonder, apprehension—and no one to share them with. Then there was the ultimate decision she had to make: whether to keep her baby or give him up for adoption. A feeling of loneliness, sadness, or perhaps some postpartum depression may have accounted for Darlene placing a touching poem on the back of her son's birth announcement.

HAVING A HUSBAND

Having a husband is diverse
with fat and lean, with better and worse,
with thick and thin, and trick and treat,
and taking the bitter with the sweet.

Having a husband is comforting, warm
as a summer wave. It's a cloud, a storm!
It's a rock on which you can depend
and a child for whom you have to fend!

It's shoulder to shoulder and side to side;
it's at opposite poles and against the tide;
it's a constant climate, a fickle weather
that can only be joined by two together!

—Helen Harrington

Chapter Twenty-Eight

Darlene checked back into St. Anthony's on St. Valentine's Day, 1962. And from the moment she got there, she began preparing to leave—both the Home and her week-old son. One nun, trained in social work, spent an hour a day with Darlene in counseling sessions. Another, based on years of experience, had developed a carefully regimented schedule for the gradual weaning of the baby away from the mother. While still in the hospital, newborns were allowed to stay with their mothers for no more than three hours a day, usually for an hour at a time—in the morning, afternoon, and evening. When the girls returned to St. Anthony's, that time was cut back to one hour, and one hour only, at night.

The sisters also kept the girls busy by having them prepare a shopping list for their newborns. When the new mothers were healthy enough, they would be driven to a local department store to shop for the things they wrote down. Darlene, a meticulous person by nature, carefully prepared her list on a little green card. It included the following:

6 blankets	2 kimonos
2 shoes	4 gowns
1 pacifier	1 towel and cloth
2 dresses	4 boots
1 apron	1 play shirt set
2 dress hats	1 sweater
2 pants	1 T shirt.

The total cost for all these items was $6.75, which she paid out of her own pocket.

After the shopping list was completed, after numerous counseling sessions, and when the sister in charge felt that Darlene was ready, formal documents were presented which legally transferred her son to Catholic Charities, Inc. On February 20, 1962, a nearby notary public was brought in to witness her signature. Among other things, the document stated: "I hereby relinquish full claim forever to my child, Bill Patrick Albert, and I hereby surrender the said child . . . and I understand never to make any claim to the said child." Other official records state:

> Darlene, as she was single and unwed, felt that it would be for the best interest and welfare of her child if consents to adoption were signed . . . Adoption procedures were explained to her and she freely and voluntarily signed [the documents of surrender].

The next morning, after mass and breakfast, one of the nuns brought little Bill Patrick Albert into a meeting room on the first floor to see his mother for the last time.

"It's time to say goodbye," she said softly.

Darlene took the baby in her arms and sat down in a rocking chair. He was dressed in one of the blue outfits she had purchased for him. She gave her son a prolonged hug, whispered "I love you" in his ear, kissed him on the cheek, and then handed him back to the nun. Then she was ushered in to see Sister Mathilde to formally check out of St. Anthony's.

The good sister presented Darlene with a final invoice. She was charged $186.45 for "Board" from September 12, 1961 through February 7, 1962, $20 for "Medicines and Miscellaneous supplies," $12.90 for "Board after Delivery from February 14, 1962 to February 20, 1962, and $150 for "Hospitalization." The total amount came to $369.35.

Sister Mathilde, seeing that Darlene still had tears in her eyes from the emotional parting with her child, got up, came around the desk, and gave Darlene a big hug. Then, for comfort, she handed her a religious card which featured a beautiful picture of the Virgin Mary on the front. Darlene thanked the nun for her gesture and walked out of St. Anthony's for the final time.

On the back of the religious card, she later wrote: "Mother," "Darlene," "'62."

The Blessed Virgin Mary is truly the Mother of God, because the same Divine Person who is the Son of God is also the Son of the Blessed Virgin Mary.

∼

On February 21, 1962—the exact same day Darlene said goodbye to her son and left St. Anthony's Infant Home—Clara Albert sat in a "Progress Evaluation Meeting" at the Larned State mental institution with her doctors.

Because she "seemed to be doing much better now," as one physician noted, Clara was "referred to a nursing home for placement." However, she was "to keep under care of the family doctor," and it was recommended that she "continue to take Thorazine spansule, 75 mg at h.s." [bedtime].

That day, Clara was transported to a nursing home and, a short time thereafter, she was back in Wichita on the farm with her parents.

Darlene never told her mother about her unwed pregnancy or the traumatic parting she had experienced with her child. But had she done so, it likely would have had a negative impact on Clara, who knew that particular pain only too well.

Chapter Twenty-Nine

Darlene rode back to Wichita on a bus by herself. She did not tell anyone she was coming—not her sister, not her mother, not any of her brothers, not Mulvihill—no one.

Upon her return, she expanded on the lie she had told people. She had been in Kansas City studying to be a nurse's assistant, she said. But things just didn't work out. She did not enjoy it as much as she thought she would. So she decided to drop out.

Darlene was certain Norma Jean would take her back in with no questions asked. But when she arrived unannounced with suitcases in hand at the Interdale apartment complex, she received a surprise. Her sister was involved with an enlisted serviceman and they were planning to be married in May. After the wedding, they were going to move to Ohio. To top it off, the apartment was already contracted out to the next occupants, so Darlene would have to find someplace else to live after the wedding.

Twenty-four-year-old Private Jerry Kerg from Dayton, Ohio, met Norma Jean Albert, age twenty-one, at the Pirate's Cave nightclub on a Saturday night. He found himself captivated by her tall, striking figure as she stood alone at the bar, so he went up and asked her to dance. The two got along well from the start and began talking about marriage within a few weeks. Jerry was stationed at McConnell Air Force base in Wichita and was slated to be discharged that summer. He had little knowledge of Norma Jean's history in the orphanage and even less about the rest of the family. All he knew was that he had found the "girl of his dreams" and was going to marry her, take her back Ohio, and raise a family. As far as he was concerned, that was all he needed to know.

So Jerry was as surprised as anyone when Darlene showed up. The only thing Norma Jean had ever told him about his future sister-in-law was that "she'd been seeing a priest," which he thought odd. He wasn't even sure what that meant. He did notice, however, that upon her return, Darlene was strangely quiet and apprehensive. Norma also observed that she no longer carried her rosary and prayer book with her everywhere she went. Nor did she seem to pray as much as she used to. Clearly, there was a major change in her personality.

Jerry and Norma Jean went out of their way to help Darlene get settled. They found her a small, one-bedroom apartment a few blocks away—put down a deposit to secure the place for occupancy in June, and then paid the first few months' rent. Next they set about helping her find a job.

"What kind of work can you do?" asked Jerry.

"Well, I'm pretty good at cleaning," replied Darlene. "I worked as a maid in the rectory for the priests since I was thirteen. The nuns really taught us to clean well at the orphanage. They pounded it into us. Said we'd need to be good at it when we got married and had children."

With that to go on, Norma Jean and Jerry lined up a job for Darlene as a maid at one of the local motels. It didn't pay very much, but at least it was something to start her out.

For the next several months, Darlene worked during the day cleaning out rooms to ready them for the evening's incoming guests. At night, she did what everybody else did back then—she headed downtown to drink and party. One of her favorite haunts was Eddie's Bar—located a short walking distance from where she lived. Darlene would go there almost every evening with some of the other girls who worked at the motel. They'd have a few drinks, chat, and then go get something to eat. Later, they'd return and mingle with the late-night crowd. After awhile, she became acquainted with the owner of Eddie's and was offered a job cleaning up the place after it closed down at 2:00 in the morning. It was perfect for her, because she could work until 4:00 or 5:00 AM, go back to her apartment, sleep until noon, and then report to work at the motel after check-out time.

Over the next several years, Darlene bounced around the downtown area taking jobs at a number of different motels. But she continued to work at Eddie's Bar. It was as steady a job as she would ever have.

Meanwhile, Norma Jean and Jerry ran off by themselves to get married. Norma Jean refused to have a church wedding and did not want any of her family present—not even Darlene. So they went out and found a local judge who performed the ceremony in his house. A friend of Jerry's and his wife stood up for them. That night, Norma Jean pleaded with her husband to leave for Ohio as soon as possible.

"Oh, Jerry, I want to get away from everything around here," she said. "I want to make a home. I want to have kids. I want a fresh start. I want to leave behind all these bad memories."

"What bad memories?" asked Jerry.

"All of them," she replied.

Chapter Thirty

Jerry and Norma Jean decided to delay their move back to Ohio until after her brother Ray's wedding in the fall. The ceremony was slated to take place in mid-November at St. Mary's Cathedral, the largest and most beautiful Catholic church in Wichita, with a grand reception and dance afterward at the downtown Knights of Columbus Hall.

Ray had met his fiancée, Carol Zimmerman, not long after returning to Wichita for his senior year in high school. He'd left Towanda in a huff after Sheriff Babcock's wife, Marie, accused him of stealing money from the family-owned grocery store. Even though Dallas chastised Marie for making such an outlandish charge, Ray felt it was best just to clear out. So he moved back to Wichita on his own and, for a time, lived with his father, Joe. Ray also landed a job at the Jennings IGA grocery store, where he made $40 a week working after school.

That's where he met Carol, who was coming through the line one day when he was at the checkout stand. Even though she was a senior at St. Mary's Catholic High School and he was over at North High, it didn't stop them from seeing each other on a regular basis. It seemed like a match made in heaven from the very beginning. Carol's parents simply loved Ray. He was polite, kind, an industrious workaholic, and extremely likable. So there were no objections raised when the two announced that they were planning on getting married after graduating from high school.

Everybody was going to be at the wedding: All the Alberts—Joe, Darlene, Norma Jean and Jerry, and the younger brothers, who were to be bused in from Boys Town. All the Martins would be there, too—Clara and her parents, Stephen and Alphonse, several cousins, aunts, and uncles. Everybody seemed willing to put their differences aside for this happy occasion—the wedding of Joe and Clara's oldest son.

Because Carol's mother and father were German—and they knew the Alberts were also of German extraction—they planned a lavish reception with German food, dance, and tradition. The ceremony went off flawlessly, and everything—the bridesmaids, the flowers, the music, all the people—was just beautiful. Afterwards, everyone drove over to the Knights of Columbus Hall in the 600 block of Broadway. When people walked in the door, they were handed their first dose of the evening's German tradition—a jigger of the best Irish whiskey Mr. Zimmerman was able to procure. Even the underage Albert boys, Roy, Donald, Gene, and Dean downed a shot—and it was one they'd never forget.

Everyone had a great time enjoying all the German food and Irish whiskey. And predictably, as time wore on, most of the men became pretty tipsy. Toward the end of the evening, Jerry walked into the men's room and overheard Stephen and Alphonse Martin and two of their cousins "cussing up a streak" about Joe Albert. And when one of them said something about "that blond-haired bastard," Jerry demanded to know if they were talking about him. But the Martin boys simply ignored him and walked out just in time to encounter Joe leaving. But Alphonse, so drunk he was actually stumbling, quickly began yelling at Joe.

"Why are you here at this wedding?" he shouted. "How could you possibly come to a function like this when you couldn't take care of your kids when it was your time and responsibility to do it? Now you want to join in the family fun, huh?"

Joe was hard-headed and tough—so tough, in fact, that he was known for pulling his own teeth by taking a fingernail file, loosening the tooth, and then yanking it out with a pair of pliers. There was no doubt he could take care of himself. But not wishing to disrupt his son's wedding, Joe just turned away and walked outside.

Carol and Ray were dancing when they heard all the ruckus and saw a bunch of people crowding up near the front door. "Why don't you stay in here, Carol," Ray said to his bride. "I'll see what's going on."

When Ray arrived up front, his father reassured him that everything would be all right after he left. "Just ignore them, son," he said. "They've had too much to drink."

"Okay, Pop. Let me walk you to your car, though."

As the two proceeded outside, they were closely followed by fifteen or twenty people—about half of them Martins, the other half Alberts. And when everybody got outside, Alphonse again began yelling at Joe.

"Joe Albert, you are a son-of-a-bitch!" he screamed. "You're a no good bastard!"

Joe ignored the name-calling and just kept walking toward his car. But Ray did not. He immediately lunged toward his uncle Alphonse and slugged him in the jaw. And that started the biggest street fight Wichita had seen in decades. People who were there described it as a "Hatfields and McCoys" brawl. Only this was Kansas instead of Kentucky. This was the Martins against the Alberts.

Jerry, who hardly knew anybody, carefully took off his glasses and handed them to Norma Jean's aunt Betty, then he jumped into the fray. But Aunt Betty put Jerry's glasses in her purse and then promptly started banging Martin men over the head with it. Everybody was swinging at each other. Ray was rolling around on the ground with Alphonse. Gene jumped onto his uncle Steve's back and started pounding him in the head. Dean tackled one of the cousins. And Norma Jean hit somebody over the head with an empty whiskey bottle while Darlene held Roy and Donald back from the fray. Only Joe did not throw any punches. He just got in his car and drove away.

Within a few minutes, sirens sounded as police cars descended from all directions on the Knights of Columbus Hall. Jerry quickly grabbed Norma Jean and ducked out the back entrance. Still in the Army, he knew if he got arrested and was found to be drinking, he'd be thrown in the stockade. But as they were headed down the back alley, a police cruiser turned in and started straight for them.

"Oh Jesus! Our goose is cooked. Just keep walking," he whispered to Norma Jean. They both breathed a sigh of relief, however, when the police car just went right on by without stopping.

Back out in front, the officers quickly gained control of the situation. "All right," said the lead policeman, "let's go down to the station and get all this straightened out."

Ray, who now had a torn shirt and bloodied lip, pulled the policeman aside and identified himself as the bridegroom. He was allowed to drive Carol home and then head down to the station where a long argument ensued between the Martins, the Alberts, and the police. Ray wanted to press charges against them. "They got drunk and ruined my wedding," he complained. But the police told him that if they were going to press charges against anyone, they'd have to book everybody who attended the reception—including Ray and his wife. "Do you want us to do that?" he was asked. Ray ended the entire matter by simply giving up. "Oh, forget it," he said at last. When he finally got back home, it was 6:00 AM so he just curled up on the couch and went to sleep.

Later that day, Ray and Carol packed up the car and drove the four boys back to Boys Town. Then they started out on their honeymoon. They didn't know where they were going to go. They just got in the car and drove. And when darkness fell, they found themselves in Wahoo, Nebraska—which is where they spent their first night as husband and wife.

"Well, this is fitting," Carol quipped to Ray as they checked into the motel.

Chapter Thirty-One

In August, 1962, Gene Albert was down in the basement of Henry's Tailor Shop in Wichita when Father Daniel Mulvihill walked in—at least he thought it was Mulvihill. Rather than being dressed like a priest, he was clad in khaki pants and a green sports shirt open at the collar. He was also smoking a big cigar.

"Hi Gene," he said in his heavy Irish accent. "I'm Daniel Mulvihill. Remember me?"

"Sure, Father. How are you?"

"Good, Gene. I heard you had gotten out of Boys Town a few months ago and then taken a job here as an apprentice. Are you enjoying it?"

"Yes, Father. It's a good job."

"Say, do you remember that fishing trip I took you and your brothers on years ago?" asked Mulvihill.

"Sure do, Father," replied Gene. "It started raining after a few hours and we all had to drive back."

"I sure enjoyed that. It was a lot of fun, wasn't it?"

"Sure was, Father."

"Say, Gene. I've been trying to locate Darlene. I understand she moved. Do you know where I can find her?"

Gene paused a moment and wondered if he should tell Mulvihill where his sister's new apartment was located. He decided against it.

"No, Father. I'm not sure where she lives now. She moved because Norma Jean got married and left for Dayton."

"Oh, yes. Norma Jean. Good for her. I'm sure she's happy."

"Yes, she is."

"Well, do you have any idea where I might find Darlene?"

"Well, she works at the Commodore Motel. You might be able to find her there. Do you know where it is, Father?"

"Just on the edge of downtown, isn't it, Gene?"

"Yes, Father."

"Well, I think I'll wander over there and see if I can find her. Haven't seen her in a long time."

"Okay, Father."

"Thank you, Gene," said Mulvihill waving his cigar as he walked out.

"You're welcome, Father."

Mulvihill headed directly over to the motel and happened to find Darlene leaving just as he got there.

"Hi sweetheart!" he called out.

Darlene seemed startled. "How did you find me?" she asked.

"I ran into your brother, Gene. He told me. Come on, let's take a walk downtown, maybe get a drink or a bite to eat."

As the two wandered down Main Street, Mulvihill noticed a photo booth where you could buy two instant black-and-white pictures for a quarter.

"Come on, this looks like fun," he said. "Let's duck in here."

Inside the small booth, Darlene sat on the priest's right knee. They took four photographs in all—and Darlene had a big smile on her face in the first two shots. For the third picture, Mulvihill leaned over and asked her for a kiss. Obligingly, she turned around and kissed him while he held up the cigar high in his left hand. Darlene's smile, however, was gone in the ensuing fourth photograph—as though she might have regretted the kiss.

The truth is that Darlene had been having grave doubts about her entire relationship with Daniel Mulvihill. Over the previous six months, ever since having the baby and returning to Wichita, he had been following her around, stalking her, insisting they continue to see each other. But when she asked if he was ever going to leave the priesthood and marry her, Mulvihill quickly changed the subject.

So, in recent months, Darlene had been trying to avoid him—not telling him where her new apartment was or where she worked. She was really upset with Gene for giving him that information. There would always be a bit of a rift between the two of them after that. And Gene could never understand why it had upset her so much.

Almost twenty-one now, Darlene began to ponder what had happened to her—and things began to weigh heavily on her mind. It began to sink in that she had had an illicit affair with a Catholic priest, that she had become pregnant, had his son, and then had given the baby up for adoption. My God, how could all that have happened, she wondered. He was supposed to leave the priesthood, marry her, get a job, raise their family together. That's what he said he was going to do. He said he loved me. Why hadn't he done it? Maybe he just wanted sex all along, she thought. Maybe that was it. Maybe that's all he wanted since she was thirteen years old. But what about her baby? What about her son, Bill Patrick? What would become of him? She might never have another child. Maybe she could get him back. Maybe she could raise him herself. But, wait, she had signed those damned documents of surrender. How could she overcome that? Maybe she could get a lawyer. But she didn't have the money for that, did she? Maybe Bill Patrick hadn't been adopted yet. Maybe she could go to Kansas City and try to get him back. Yeah. Maybe she'd do that.

A few weeks after Darlene's twenty-first birthday, on December 3, 1962, an opportunity to return to Kansas City presented itself. Mary Kay Hallacy, a girlfriend she had first met while a freshman at Walnut High School back in 1958, had called to say she had just moved to Kansas City to take a new job and was lonely.

"Why don't you come up for a visit?" suggested Mary Kay. "We can go out and have some fun."

Darlene jumped at the chance. She purchased a round-trip bus ticket and, on a Sunday, rode over to Kansas City for a planned week-long stay. Mary Kay met her at the bus station, and the two went out shopping, had lunch, and reminisced about old times. That evening, they drove around for hours looking at all the beautiful Christmas lights in neighborhood after neighborhood.

The next morning, Darlene mentioned that she had something to do, and that she had to do it by herself.

"Can I drive you somewhere on my way to work?" asked Mary Kay.

"Oh, no thanks. I'll take the bus."

"Okay. There's a bus stop just around the corner. They run every fifteen minutes or so. I'll see you back here at 5:30 and we'll have dinner."

Darlene got on the bus and asked the driver the best way to get to East 27th Street. It was her lucky day, he told her. She'd only have to make one transfer, and she would be there lickety-split.

Thirty minutes later, Darlene was let off half a block from St. Anthony's Infant Home at 1414 East 27th Street. As she walked up the street, she began thinking about what was going on inside. The children were all up by now. They had eaten and been dressed. Bill Patrick was ten months old. He was probably in the play area right now. They might be taking him outside to play in a few minutes. Wonder if he's walking yet. Wait a minute, I wonder if he's there at all. Maybe he's not. Maybe he's already been adopted out.

The closer Darlene got to St. Anthony's, the slower she walked. Finally, she stopped altogether at the corner directly across the street from the back of the Home. And there she waited. One hour. Two hours. Three hours. Longer. Several toddlers were brought outside at various times to play in the backyard. Darlene strained to catch a glimpse of any little boy that might look to be Bill Patrick. But she couldn't recognize him. Unable to work up enough courage to go inside, she finally decided that it was no use.

So Darlene got back on a bus and rode around town for a while. At some point, she got off and wandered into a bar. When she arrived back at her girlfriend's apartment around 6:00, Mary Kay could tell she had been drinking.

"Are you okay?" she asked.

"I gotta get back to Wichita," replied Darlene. "Will you please drive me to the bus station? I'm leaving now."

Chapter Thirty-Two

For their first Christmas as a married couple together, Jerry gave Norma Jean a beautiful new coat. And his bride was thrilled. She had never owned a coat that nice. Actually, she told him, she had never had anything that new or that nice. For the next week, Norma Jean wore it every day. After returning home from errands, she lingered around the house with it on. Later, when the couple went out to a New Year's Eve party, she was very careful not to let it get dirty as she got into the car. Jerry remembered her picking specks of lint off so it would look perfect when they arrived.

At the party, however, Norma Jean tossed the coat on a bed and forgot about it. She began drinking heavily and, by midnight, was stumbling around and screaming obscenities at a couple of people she did not particularly like. At 12:15, Jerry decided he'd better get her out of there. But his wife didn't want to go. She was having a good time, she said. Why was he such a stick-in-the-mud? And when he insisted they leave, and leave now, she began cursing at him, too. At last, he persuaded his wife to put her coat on and then guided her out to the car.

Jerry was greatly relieved when he finally pulled up in front of his own house. "Whew! I got her home before she got sick," he thought to himself. But as he turned off the engine, Norma Jean vomited all over the place—on the front seat, on the dashboard, and on her new coat. The next morning, hung over and hazy about what had happened, Norma Jean cried when she saw the damage she had done to her coat. The stains and the smell were just awful. And she was so pained by the experience that she never wore the coat again.

It didn't take long for Jerry to notice that Norma Jean's behavior on New Year's Eve was part of a recurring pattern. She'd go over to a friend's house, drink too much, become verbally abusive, and then get sick. One particularly embarrassing incident occurred at the home of Jerry's parents right after they had arrived in Ohio. Norma Jean got so drunk that she fell off her chair at the dining room table and could not get up by herself. When her father-in-law tried to help her up, she cursed him "a blue streak."

Jerry didn't find out Norma Jean had a drinking problem until after they were married. She had effectively hidden it from him while they were in Wichita. But because he really loved her, he worked with her to try and cure the ailment. First, he helped her secure a job as an X-ray technician at a Dayton medical facility. It was familiar and comforting to her, because it was essentially the same thing she'd been doing when they first met. Jerry also focused Norma Jean on trying to build a home and family. He himself got a job at a successful barber shop and built a three-bedroom house on some acreage out in Randolph Township, just north of the city. They cultivated new friends, new neighbors, and tried hard to have a baby. But Norma Jean had trouble conceiving. Distressed and worried, she called her mother in Wichita to talk about it. But Clara was reassuring. "Don't be concerned," she said, "the same thing happened to me. It took several years before I finally got pregnant—and then look how many kids we ended up having. Just keep trying."

Over the next year or so, everything appeared to be working out fairly well. Norma Jean stopped drinking and settled into a comfortable married life. Jerry was as happy as he'd ever been. But just before they were preparing to go on a vacation, Norma Jean, who had recently undergone the yearly free physical offered by her employer, received a call from her doctor.

"I don't want you to go anywhere," he told her. "Our X rays show a cyst on one of your ovaries, and I want to check it out to make sure it's benign and not growing."

So they put off their vacation and Norma Jean checked into the hospital the following week for exploratory surgery. During the operation, Jerry paced back and forth apprehensively in the waiting room for five long hours. Finally, the doctor came out and told him that Norma Jean's cyst was actually a tumor that had grown significantly since the first X ray. It was obvious that his wife had ovarian cancer, he said.

"We had to perform a total hysterectomy," the doctor told him. "It was the only thing to do."

"What's the prognosis?" Jerry asked.

"Good," the physician replied. "We think we got it all. But she'll have to undergo radiation treatment right away to make sure. And of course, Mr. Kerg, you realize that she'll never be able to have a baby."

Jerry's knees buckled when he heard that last part. He knew that his wife would have a major problem with not being able to have kids. It would probably impact her more than the cancer. But at that moment, the cancer was what Jerry was most afraid of. My God, he thought, what would he do if she died? It was too much to even contemplate.

Jerry was correct about Norma Jean's reaction. After the surgery, she was distraught, inconsolable—at times, even hysterical. Undergoing radiation treatment only served to make things worse. As her hair fell out and she became nauseous and sick to her stomach, Norma Jean sunk into a deep depression that alternated between severe melancholia and suicidal tendencies. She had to be kept sedated much of the time.

After the treatment was completed and Norma Jean began to recover, the doctors were optimistic about her physical condition. "We think she's beaten the cancer," one of them told Jerry. "Time will tell on that. But psychologically, she's having some major problems."

"What should we do?"

"Well, we want to examine her regularly to make certain the disease doesn't return. And it would be a good idea to put her under the care of a psychiatrist—at least until she begins to show signs of improvement."

Norma Jean returned to her job several months later. But coworkers observed noticeable differences in her demeanor. They saw a forlorn look in her face, a general apathy toward work, and an unwillingness to engage in any kind of meaningful conversation. Jerry, meanwhile, became alarmed that his wife had started drinking again—at times, heavily. Each night when he got home, he could smell alcohol on her breath. And each night, she would pester him about adoption.

"I want to adopt a child, got to adopt a child, must adopt a child," she would say over and over again. Finally, Jerry relented and agreed to see what could be done. But because he was concerned about Norma Jean's ability to raise a child in her current mental state, he consulted privately with the psychiatrist.

"What do you think?" he asked the doctor.

"Jerry, I'd let her go through with it," came the reply. "Go ahead and put your name in. It will take you two years before you could finalize the adoption, anyway. Let's see how Norma Jean does during that time. If she comes out of this depression and stops her drinking, everything might work out just fine. If she doesn't . . . well, there's just no way you'd be allowed to adopt a child."

Chapter Thirty-Three

In January, 1963, one month after Darlene stood outside St. Anthony's Infant Home hoping to catch a glimpse of her son, a young couple in Kansas City received a call from a caseworker with the local Catholic Charities.

"I have some good news for you," she said. "We've found a child that matches your profile."

"Oh, good," replied the delighted Mary Smith [name changed].

"It's a boy, eleven months old," continued the caseworker. "Father has Irish roots, the mother, a German heritage just like you. His name is Bill Patrick. He's a very healthy child. Only one small problem. He can't walk just yet. His legs are bowed and he has to wear braces for a year or so. Other than that, he's in excellent health, and I believe he's perfect for you."

"Well, that sounds wonderful. What do we do now?"

"Why don't you and your husband travel to see us, and we'll introduce you to him?"

"Okay, we'll be there."

Mary and Jim Smith [names changed] had been married for about five years. They were a fine young couple who wanted very much to raise a family. But they had been told by their physician that it was not possible for them to conceive on their own. Devoutly Catholic, the two consulted with their parish priest and, when he recommended that they pursue an adoption through the Catholic church, they did not hesitate to do so. After filling out all the necessary paperwork and waiting patiently for about three months, the caseworker's call finally came.

Excited and a bit apprehensive, Mary and Jim journeyed to St. Anthony's Infant Home in Kansas City to meet their prospective new son. Sister Mathilde greeted the couple at the door and showed them to a small room on the first floor, where the caseworker was already waiting. A few minutes later, Sister Mathilde returned with the little boy in her arms.

"Mr. and Mrs. Smith," said the nun, "Let me introduce you to Bill Patrick."

The child immediately grinned broadly at Mary and reached out his arms for her. And that was all it took. In a few minutes, Jim looked over at the caseworker.

"What do we have to do to make this happen?" he asked.

"You'll have to file a petition for adoption which, if accepted—and I fully expect it will be accepted—will allow you to take Bill Patrick home with you while a more formal review is conducted."

"A review?" asked Jim.

"Yes, Mr. Smith. There are strict procedures we must follow to check into both of your backgrounds as well as verify that of the child's. Nothing to be concerned about. It's in everybody's best interests, I assure you."

"Well, okay. Let's start the process," said Jim. "I'll have our attorney call you this afternoon."

Formal filing of the petition for adoption began, and while the application was under review, Bill Patrick Albert was placed in the care and custody of the Smiths in a formal foster care relationship.

In the meantime, the Catholic Charities of the Diocese of Kansas City-St. Joseph, Missouri, assigned another case social worker to conduct an exhaustive investigation into the suitability of the Smiths and their commitment to raising the child in the Catholic faith. Specifically, according to procedures and rules, the adoptive parents had to be "of the same religion as the child and his parents or, if the child is illegitimate, his mother"—and that "a child's rights in respect of faith and morals must be protected by such safeguards as well as assure his adoption by persons who profess the religion of the child." The prospective parents also had to swear that they were "not delib-

erately shirking natural conception," and they had to promise
to bring the child up in the Catholic faith and educate him in
Catholic schools.

Nine months later a formal proceeding was held for a decree
of adoption. According to the official record,

> [The caseworker], heretofore appointed guardian *ad litem*
> for said minor child, has made an investigation relative to
> the Petitioners in this cause . . . [and affirms] that he finds
> them to be of good reputation and moral character and
> that they have the ability and means to care for and edu-
> cate said child; and said guardian has filed his answer
> herein to such effect and recommending that the best
> interest of said minor child would be served by the grant-
> ing of this adoption.

In addition, the report noted that a full and complete investigation has been made of the physical and mental conditions and
the antecedents of said child as to its suitability for adoption by the
Catholic Charities of the Diocese of Kansas City-St. Joseph, Missouri . . . an agency duly engaged in the care and placement of
children in family homes within the meaning of the provisions of
Section 453.070 of the Revised Statutes of Missouri, 1959.

Then, with the following words, the adoption of Darlene
Albert's son was made formal and final:

> Wherefore, it is ordered, adjudged and decreed, that said
> minor child, Bill Patrick Albert . . . shall, to all legal intents
> and purposes, be the child of said Petitioners . . . as if born
> to them in lawful wedlock, that the name of said minor
> child be and it is hereby changed from Bill Patrick Albert
> to T. J. Smith [name changed], and that the natural par-
> ents of said child shall in no wise hereafter have any right
> or claim to or for the services, wages, custody, control or
> company of said child . . .
>
> The written consent of the natural mother, duly exe-
> cuted and acknowledged, consenting to the adoption
> herein, has been filed with this Court.
>
> Petitioners pay the cost of this proceeding and $50 to
> [the caseworker] for his services.

Right about this time, Darlene Albert was fired from her job at Eddie's Bar in Wichita for being drunk on the job. The owner had warned her about it the week before, when it had happened the first time. If she showed up that way one more time, he'd said, that would be it—and Eddie was a man of his word.

Darlene's uncle Stephen quickly arranged employment for her as a cleaning person at Beech Aircraft where he worked. But after only one week, Darlene abruptly walked off the job—leaving her lunch box and cleaning materials behind. She did not even inform her boss or her uncle that she had quit.

Over the next three months, Darlene continued to drink heavily. She closed down the local bars at night, slept during the day, and was unable to hold down any kind of a job. Having trouble making ends meet, she finally went on public assistance in April, 1964.

Chapter Thirty-Four

"Jerry, there's something wrong with Norma Jean," said Mary.

"What do you mean?"

"She's just not acting right. She's either in a daze most of the time or she's hallucinating."

Mary had just returned from a short vacation to Florida with Norma Jean. It was supposed to be a "girls' vacation"—a time away from the husbands. But it turned out to be a nightmare. They were gone only a couple of days when Mary was awakened in the middle of the night by a frantic Norma Jean pacing back and forth across the motel room and shouting: "I can see again! I can see again!" At first, Mary thought her friend had been walking in her sleep. But then she realized that was not the case. Norma Jean was wide awake. She was raving about this and that, claiming to be someone named "Myrna," and just generally acting out of her mind. Alarmed, Mary immediately called a halt to the vacation and hastily headed back to Dayton.

When they pulled into the Kerg's driveway the next day, Norma Jean was alternately asleep or babbling nonsense. Jerry quickly called his wife's psychiatrist and asked him to come over to the house as soon as possible. Later that afternoon, after conducting an extensive examination, the physician finally emerged from the back bedroom.

"Jerry, I don't mean to alarm you," he said, "but I think Norma Jean is schizophrenic. We've got to put her in the hospital right away. And I mean right now."

"Okay, doctor," Jerry replied. "Whatever it takes."

Within twenty-four hours, Norma Jean Albert Kerg was committed to the psychiatric ward of St. Elizabeth's Hospital in Dayton, Ohio. At first, she was put on high doses of medication designed to alleviate her symptoms and hallucinogenic behavior. But when she failed to respond, her doctor ordered extensive electric shock treatment. While this radical method was commonly used to treat depression and schizophrenia from the late 1930s through the 1950s, in the late 1960s it was reserved only for the most extreme cases and only when new antipsychotic drugs failed to work. In Norma Jean's case, doctors had hoped the loss of memory, which often accompanied electric shock treatment, might be beneficial.

For the next six months, Norma Jean was kept in a locked, padded cell and treated with alternating high doses of powerful drugs and intermittent pulses of electricity to the brain. Jerry, however, was beside himself with anguish. He just couldn't stand to see his wife in such a state. Frustrated that he wasn't seeing any improvement, Jerry finally decided to make a change. He hired a new psychiatrist and transferred Norma Jean to the Miami Valley Hospital. There, the frequency of shock treatment was cut back and new drugs were prescribed. At first, she seemed to do a little better. At least she could recognize him once in a while which, to Jerry, was a significant improvement. He had gone a long time without even so much as a "hello" from his wife. However, her periods of normalcy were infrequent and her progress slow.

Eventually, Jerry's insurance ran out and he was forced to transfer Norma Jean to the Ohio State Mental Hospital in Dayton—where her care and treatment would now be paid for by the state. It tore Jerry up to sign the orders of commitment, but he had no other choice. Surprisingly, though, Norma Jean's condition improved almost immediately. The state doctors decided to cut way back on her daily intake of drugs and eliminate the electric shock treatment altogether. Within days, Norma Jean was talking, smiling, eating, and, all-in-all, acting like her old self. Three months later, she was given a clean bill of health and released—although cautioned to make certain that she strictly adhered to the new regime of drugs the doctors had prescribed.

By the time 1970 rolled around, Norma Jean was doing fairly well. The new decade found her back at work, enjoying her friends, and fairly happy in her marriage. Still, however, there were periodic bouts with depression, but the psychiatrist said that was to be expected. During one of those melancholy moods, Norma Jean said she wanted to go back to Wichita to see her mother and father. And Jerry thought it might be a good idea for her to be around family again. He especially believed she might enjoy being with Darlene. So they drove back to Kansas for a weeklong vacation.

Overall, Jerry was right. Seeing her parents and brothers really picked up Norma Jean's spirits. She and Darlene particularly spent a lot of time together, mostly going out to bars and drinking. They had such a good time, though, that when it came time to return home, Norma Jean didn't want to leave. As a matter of fact, she threw a fit. When Jerry began to drive away from their motel, Norma Jean opened the door and tried to jump out of the car while it was moving. He managed to grab her, stop the car, and pull her back in. Then he got her back into the motel room.

Unsure of what to do next, Jerry called brothers Ray and Gene for help. When Ray got there about an hour later, he found Norma Jean unresponsive and almost completely unable to do anything for herself except talk—which she did incoherently and incessantly. She didn't want to go back to Ohio, she said. She wanted to stay home with her mother and father. She wanted to be with her sister. She wanted to live like a real family. She wanted kids of her own. And she'd kill anyone who ever tried to take them away. She didn't like Jerry. Jerry was out to get her. Please help her, Ray. Let her stay in Wichita.

Alarmed, Ray suggested they drive Norma Jean to the local hospital right away. Jerry quickly agreed and got behind the wheel while Ray sat in the backseat and held his sister. She wanted to be hugged, but she didn't want her husband to touch her.

"She must've stopped taking her medicine," said Jerry at one point. "Hell, she might even have thrown it out. I can't find any of it."

"Well, let's see if the doctors will give her some more at the hospital."

Gene showed up at the hospital later that morning. He had to get permission to get off work at the post office or he would have been there sooner.

In the waiting room, the doctors informed Jerry, Ray, and Gene that Norma Jean was now quiet. They had given her a strong drug to calm her down. She could travel back to Ohio, he said, but should be hospitalized as soon as she got there.

"I don't know how I'm going to get her back to Dayton," said Jerry. "I'm afraid she might try to jump out of the car again. Then what do I do if she hurts herself?"

"Well, maybe I can take a few days off work and ride back with you," said Gene.

"Are you sure you want to do that?" asked Jerry. "That's your vacation time."

"Well, this is family," he replied. "This is more important than any vacation."

So Gene made the long drive back to Ohio. While Jerry drove, he sat in the backseat with his older sister. And most of the way, she slept in his arms.

When they arrived, Jerry drove Gene to the airport and paid for his plane trip back to Wichita. Then he checked Norma Jean into the mental ward at Good Samaritan Hospital. The doctors immediately prescribed three days' worth of electric shock treatment and told Jerry that his wife must never again touch another drop of alcohol.

"She's just not all there, Mr. Kerg," said the doctor. "She's just not there."

Chapter Thirty-Five

Knock. Knock. Knock.

"Hello, Darlene? Darlene? It's your brother, Gene."

Knock. Knock. Knock.

"Come on, Darlene. I've got our mother with me. We've come to visit you. Open the door, will you?"

"Maybe she's not in there," said Clara.

"No, Mother," responded Gene. "She's there. She just never answers the door."

Knock. Knock. Knock.

"Darlene! Darlene! It's your mother. Come on, baby. Come to the door."

Knock. Knock. Knock.

"Well, I guess we'd better go," said Gene, finally. "Doesn't look like she's going to answer. Let's try again next week."

But Darlene wouldn't answer her apartment door the following week, either. She wouldn't answer it for her brothers, Dean or Ray, or anybody else who knocked. None of her family members could quite understand why, but Darlene was becoming more and more reclusive with each passing year. She just didn't want to see anybody—especially Father Daniel Mulvihill, who was still pursuing her, although less frequently than in the past. He had again, for instance, showed up at Gene's place of work and inquired about Darlene's whereabouts. Again wearing street clothes, Mulvihill said he had become a pilot and was looking for Darlene to take her up for a spin. Gene stated matter-of-factly he could not give him any information—that he knew she had moved but he didn't know where. Mulvihill then became irritated, even a bit angry.

"Why won't you tell me where she is, Gene? Haven't we always been friends?"

"Sorry, Father. I just can't help you."

"Where in hell is she, dammit?" yelled the priest. "I need to find her."

Gene just stared back with a blank expression on his face until Mulvihill finally left. And that was the last time any member of the Albert family ever saw or heard from him again.

To avoid the Irish priest, Darlene moved through a series of apartments in the 1960s—each only four or five blocks from downtown Wichita. From there, she walked everywhere, never driving anywhere; in fact, she didn't own a car. As far as her family knew, she did little else but cruise the local bars. In the evenings, people passed her coming or going. Sometimes she was drunk. Sometimes she'd just had a few. But, almost always, she was dressed in black and moving in a hurry as if to give the impression that she didn't have time to stop and talk. It was apparent to all of her friends that Darlene was living a tortured existence—drowning her sorrows in a bottle, carrying a grudge, mourning something or other.

One friend, Louie Rodriguez, worked at the post office with Gene. He had met Darlene many times at a downtown bar, but always in a group of people. Naturally shy, Louie was working his way up to asking her out for a date when an incident occurred that made him realize that she might have some serious psychological problems.

A bunch of guys from the post office were drinking together at one of the bars when Darlene walked in and came over to them.

"Hi there, Louie," she said as she put her arm around him and sat down. "How ya doin'?"

Louie could tell she was already pretty tipsy, so he smiled and offered to buy her a cup of coffee.

"Nope," she responded. "I'll have a beer."

Darlene then began to talk up a blue streak about anything and everything. At times she was emotional, at other times, stoic. But mostly, the guys at the table couldn't make out exactly what she was saying. It was babble. It just didn't make any sense.

After awhile, she became quiet and put her head down on the table. Louie thought she had either gone to sleep or passed out. But ten minutes later, Darlene jumped up and knocked all the beer bottles off the table and "all over creation."

"You sons of bitches aren't going to ignore me, goddammit!" she screamed. "Who the hell do you think you are?"

Darlene would frequently get a filthy mouth when she had been drinking heavily, but this was the first time Louie had ever heard her talk that way.

"Calm down, Darlene," he said. "Nobody's trying to ignore you. We just thought you were asleep. That's all."

Even though Louie thought Darlene was a beautiful young woman, after that episode he hesitated about asking her out. And when, the following week, she mentioned something about engaging in prostitution, he completely abandoned any thought of dating her. Louie never did know for sure whether Darlene had fallen into that kind of a lifestyle. But he could see how it might happen. She didn't have a job and was on public assistance. She also frequented the bars at night and often left with men she'd just met. It might be easy for her to accept a few dollars after a tryst. It might also be easy for her to find herself in some dangerous situations.

Gene Albert had no idea what kind of lifestyle his sister was engaged in when he received a call from the police one summer's night in 1971. Darlene was in the county hospital, said the officer. Somebody had broken a whiskey bottle across her face and she had to have forty stitches to close the wound. She was also drunk, the officer said, and all they could get out of her was his name and phone number.

Gene immediately dropped everything and went over to the hospital. He was shocked when he found that she was not in the emergency room, but was being held in the mental ward under lock and key.

"My God," he said to the doctor in charge. "What happened?"

"We don't know for certain, Mr. Albert. But the police were so concerned for her mental capacity that they brought her straight here. Seems she was out on the street screaming obscenities and all kinds of wild things about somebody being out to get her or something like that."

"Well, what do we do now?"

"When the alcohol wears off, she'll probably be all right and you can take her home. No one has pressed charges—nor has anyone come forward to explain what happened."

Gene was there the next morning when Darlene woke up. She was surprised to see him and could not remember anything about what had taken place the night before. When he explained what he knew, she began to cry. Then she confessed to him that she was having trouble making ends meet. Nothing had worked out like she had planned, she said. Nothing.

Gene didn't ask any questions. He just took Darlene home and nursed her back to health. When she finally got back on her feet and wanted to return to her apartment, Gene gave her a weekly stipend for food and lodging.

"I don't know why you're doing this for me," she said to him at one point.

"Because you're my sister, Darlene," he replied. "And I love you."

Chapter Thirty-Six

Darlene responded positively to her brother's act of kindness and for awhile she and Gene spent a lot of time together. But one hot summer's night, while they were bar-hopping together in downtown Wichita, Gene tried gently to slow his sister's pace of chugging beers.

"Slow down, Sis," he said. "We've got all night."

Darlene, however, ignored the advice and just kept plowing them down.

"Have you heard from Norma Jean recently?" asked Gene at one point.

"Yeah, she's a mess," came the response.

"Why? What's going on?"

"She can't have children now—you know, because of the operation. She's depressed. Drinking a lot."

"Gosh, that doesn't sound good. Maybe we can go up and visit her."

"And you know, of course, that Norma Jean was attacked when she was in the orphanage."

"Jesus, Darlene," said a startled Gene. "You mean sexually?"

"Yeah, it was one of the older boys. The sisters just laughed it off. Said she probably deserved it."

"Oh Christ!"

Just then, Darlene's eyes widened as she noticed her father walk into the bar with a woman she'd never seen before. Jumping up from the table, Darlene went straight toward Joe.

"Why, hello, Darlene," her father said with a smile. "I'd like to introduce you to Gladys. She's . . ."

"Why in hell are you going out with another woman!" Darlene screamed. "What about my mother? What do you think you're doing, you son-of-a-bitch! I think you should . . ."

At that moment, Gene grabbed his sister's arm and spun her around.

"Darlene! Darlene!" he shouted in an attempt to snap her out of her frenzy. "He's out having a good time just like we are. Settle down. It's okay. Let's just leave him alone."

"The hell with you!" Darlene shouted back. "The hell with both of you!" Then she stomped out of the bar and rushed back to her apartment.

The first thing she did when she got back was to call her sister. "You won't believe what just happened," Darlene screamed into the phone as she began to relate her story.

After listening for a few minutes, Norma Jean shocked her sister by abruptly announcing that she was in the middle of a divorce.

"What?" asked Darlene. "How come?"

"I've been seeing another guy," she responded. "Besides, Jerry and I don't get along anymore. He hates me."

The sad truth, though, was that Jerry had done everything he could to salvage the marriage and that Norma Jean was the cause of most of her own problems. After being released from the state mental institution, her depression intensified. Her drinking also increased, and when that happened, she would lose her temper over nothing and go into fits of rage. Three times she had pulled a gun on Jerry and threatened him. She would also disappear for days at a time without telling anyone where she was going.

Jerry was at the end of his rope when Norma Jean returned home late one night after a three-day absence. She tried to be quiet by getting undressed in the living room, but Jerry heard her and came out of the bedroom.

"What's going on?" he said quietly.

"I haven't been drinking. I haven't been drinking," she repeated.

"I know you haven't been drinking. I can tell that. But we've got to get all this straightened out."

"Well, I've been running around on you," confessed Norma Jean.

"I figured as much."

After a long pause. Jerry asked her what she wanted to do.

"Well, I guess I want a divorce."

Jerry swallowed hard.

"Well, do you want me to file or do you want to file?" he said at last.

"I want you to file."

"Okay, I'll take care of it tomorrow."

The next day, Norma Jean moved out of the house and Jerry started the divorce proceedings. It took six weeks to finalize everything. Norma Jean got most of the furniture, the car, and nearly all the cash—about $10,000 in all. Jerry got the house he'd worked so hard to build—and that was all right with her. She never wanted to live there after she found out she couldn't have children, anyway. She just didn't see the point.

Norma Jean stayed in Dayton for about a year after the divorce. She took a small efficiency apartment, quit her job, and continued to drink heavily. She also haunted the bars at all hours, frequently buying drinks all around, bad mouthing her ex-husband, and leaving with a different guy every night.

Every now and then, she'd drop by to see Jerry—but that occurred only when she was drunk or when she wanted something. The last time Norma Jean visited, she walked through the front door without knocking—and left the guy she'd brought with her sitting alone in the car.

She didn't have any more money, Norma Jean told Jerry. She'd blown the entire $10,000. Jerry said he was broke, too. And after a few minutes, Norma Jean's friend got tired of waiting and came to the door to see if she was ready to leave.

"He doesn't have any money, either," Jerry heard Norma Jean say as she walked back to the car. And that was the last time he ever saw her.

A few weeks later, Darlene took the bus up to Dayton to spend some time with her sister. Norma Jean was glad to see her, but there seemed to be some distance between the two of them now. They went out drinking a couple of times but had trouble speaking to each other. Unhappy with the tension, Norma Jean called Gene and asked him to come visit for a few days and bring their mother. But when he and Clara showed up, Darlene was visibly displeased. She was still mad at Gene for taking their father's side in the bar.

Everybody went out to dinner that first night, but an argument ensued when Gene began scolding Norma Jean about her dating habits. "Norma, you shouldn't take these men out and buy them liquor," he lectured. "If they're any good at all, they should pay. And you should never go out with a married man." Both sisters reacted angrily and verbally assaulted Gene. "Who do you think you are, telling us what to do?" they said.

The next morning, Darlene got up about 6:00 AM, packed her bag, and left. She didn't tell anyone where she was going and she didn't say goodbye. She just disappeared.

Chapter Thirty-Seven

Nobody heard from Darlene or knew her whereabouts for several months. And when she finally did resurface, it was only an occasional sighting by one of the brothers at one of the local Wichita bars. Gene, for example, would run into her every now and then and try to say hello. But when Darlene saw him, she'd look down as if she were ashamed and then abruptly turn and walk away. One thing he was able to observe, however, was that his sister's drinking had increased to the point that nearly every time he saw her, she was drunk. And she also seemed to have a bevy of men to hang around with—often leaving a bar with one or more of them at closing time.

One of those men, Tom Groetken, worked at the post office with Gene. Tom was a likable enough guy, a real friendly sort. He hailed from a small farming community in Iowa, served in the Army during World War II, and had moved to Wichita in 1949—the very year the Albert children were first removed from their parents' custody. Tom was thirty-two years older than Darlene and had been married once before. His first wife died suddenly under mysterious circumstances. And even though Gene knew the police had conducted an investigation and cleared Tom in the death, he was always a bit wary of this man's involvement with his sister.

Eventually, Darlene moved in with Tom, and he became her sole source of support. With time, their lifestyle became very predictable, almost ritualistic. During the day, Tom would go to work at the post office and Darlene would stay home. But at night, the two of them would prowl Wichita's downtown bars, drink heavily, and often get into trouble with the police.

Over a two-year period, from September 1968 to April 1970 for instance, Tom and/or Darlene were arrested on drunk and disorderly charges nearly a dozen times. Tom always gave the fictitious names, John P. Brost or Donald E. Lieurance, while Darlene used the name, Janet Wheeler—the same alias she'd given when she went away to have her baby at St. Anthony's Infant Home in Kansas City. And, as was her habitual nature, Darlene very meticulously cut out announcements of the arrests from the local newspaper and pasted them on index cards, which she then placed into her photo album for safekeeping. One card documented four of her brushes with the law and one of Tom's:

September 21, 1968	Janet F. Wheeler, drunk; $25 and costs.
September 3, 1968	John P. Brost, drunk, $25 and costs; failure to appear, 30 days; paroled on costs.
October 9, 1969	Janet F. Wheeler, drunk; $35 and costs.
January 22, 1970	Janet F. Wheeler, drunk, $35 and costs.
February 18, 1970	Janet F. Wheeler, drunk, $35 and costs.

One night during this period of time, Darlene ducked into a little hole-in-the-wall diner at the intersection of Harry St. and Broadway in downtown Wichita. It was well past midnight after a big night of drinking, and she was hungry. She'd tried to coax Tom into going with her, but drunk and uninterested, he walked home by himself.

Darlene had just taken her first sip of coffee when, much to her surprise, her brother Donald walked in. She quickly waved him over to take a seat at her table. "Haven't seen you in forever, Donald," said Darlene with a smile. "What've you been doing?"

Donald explained that he had just finished a night on the town with their brother, Roy. "Just thought I'd drop in to grab a quick bite," he said, grinning back at her. "Roy wasn't hungry."

Donald and Roy were the last two Albert brothers to graduate from Boys Town. Both initially moved back to Wichita, but Roy had just enlisted in the Army and was headed for an assignment in Germany—which was why they were out celebrating. Donald, on the other hand, elected to stick around and was lucky enough to land a job as a clerk at the Cudahay Meat Packing Company.

"What've you been doing, Darlene?" asked Donald.

"Drinking," she responded. "I'm real drunk, or can't you tell?"

"Well, I figured you had a few."

"Listen, here, Donald," said Darlene in a most serious tone, "Don't tell anyone in the family about me—that you saw me drinking, or eating in here, or anything. Do you hear?"

"Well, why not?"

"I just don't want you to tell anybody anything about me. Please, Donald."

"Okay, Darlene. I won't say anything."

For the next hour or so, the two had something to eat, drank several cups of coffee—and Darlene just poured her heart out. She talked and talked about everything—about Tom, about the family, about her "screwed-up life," as she phrased it. And then, all of a sudden, she grabbed her brother's arm.

"Don, I had a baby by a Catholic priest!" she said.

Stunned by his sister's revelation, Donald just sat there in silence. He couldn't say anything.

"Did you hear me, Don? I said had a baby by a Catholic priest!"

"Yes, I heard you," he finally replied pulling her next to him and hugging her tight. "My God, Darlene! My God!"

Then Darlene broke down and sobbed in her brother's arms.

Chapter Thirty-Eight

Ray was sitting at the back of the bus, head resting against the window, when the bus driver put a hand on his shoulder and shook him.

"Hey, wake up buddy, this is the end of the line. You'll have to get off now."

The driver thought the guy he was shaking was a bum. His hair was disheveled and uncombed, he had a scraggly beard, and obviously hadn't had a shower in about a week.

"Yeah, all right," said Ray, who staggered off the bus and went into the terminal. Then he curled up on a bench and went back to sleep.

A month earlier, Ray had packed everything he could fit into a small canvas suitcase and left Wichita bound for nowhere. He just rode around from town to town, sleeping in the terminals at night, getting on another bus in the morning and letting it take him wherever it happened to be going. He just wanted to start his life over—to go somewhere and get his head straight.

Ray had achieved a great deal at an early age. He had been respected in the grocery business for having climbed the corporate ladder at Mr. D's Supermarkets, to a point where he was in charge of several large grocery stores. Then, in 1971, he had taken his savings and purchased a store in Heston, Kansas, just thirty-five miles north of Wichita. His personal life had also been going well. He and Carol had owned a nice house on the west side of Wichita and were raising a family—a daughter, Melinda, and a son, Scott. Everyone had liked and respected Ray Albert. He was a good father, a good provider.

But right after he quit Mr. D's and went out on his own, things began to turn sour. Maybe it was related to the added stress of having his own business—or perhaps time, itself, was a factor. But whatever the cause, it was clear that Ray's personality was changing. And he was acting increasingly as if he were carrying around a ticking time bomb that was set to go off at any moment. He would become angry and violent whenever Carol tried to talk to him about his family's past. He grew increasingly despondent thinking about his mother's and sisters' mental problems. Somehow, it was his fault, he believed. In general, Carol always realized that Ray was suppressing a lot of angry feelings. But she was completely unprepared when the bomb finally exploded.

First, Ray stopped talking to her altogether. Next he took an apartment in Heston and stayed away from home during the week. Then he stopped coming home on the weekends, too. When Carol surprised him one weekend by driving up with the kids, she discovered he was involved with another woman.

Ray quickly ended the affair, moved out of his apartment in Heston, sold his grocery store, and went back to managing a store in Wichita. But things never really got back to normal. And Carol felt like there was an entirely different person living in her house. She didn't know Ray anymore. He didn't laugh, rarely smiled, and his behavior was erratic and unpredictable.

Without telling Carol or the children, he'd disappear for two to three weeks at a time, taking all his clothes with him. Then he'd return home just as unexpectedly and act as if nothing had happened. Things finally got to a point where it was negatively affecting the children. They'd come home after school and run in to the master bedroom to see if their father's clothes were in the closet. The third time Ray disappeared, Carol told him not to come back. It was over, she said. She wanted a divorce.

That announcement sent Ray into a full-blown depression. In fact, he almost had a nervous breakdown. There was something seriously wrong with him, he believed. He had failed at marriage. He couldn't keep his family together. Now his wife would not have a husband and his children would grow up without a father at home. My God, he thought, that's what happened to his brothers and sisters. He couldn't keep them together all those years ago—and he never managed to get them out of the orphanage as he vowed he'd do.

"What a failure I am," he said to himself. "I was supposed to be the head of the family. I was supposed keep everybody together and happy. And I didn't do any of it."

Unable to live with himself, Ray quit his job and hit the road. After a month of riding around the country on buses, he decided to head to Tucson, Arizona. A guy he used to work for was running a grocery store down there, he remembered. Why not look him up and see if he could get a job. But when he got to Tucson, he couldn't find his old boss. So he slept on park benches and sidewalks for awhile. And when he went looking for a job—any job—he had trouble. No one wanted to hire what he had become—a transient, a bum, a loser.

Then Ray decided to head out to San Francisco, where Roy was now living. Maybe he would like California, he thought. Maybe there would be a great job waiting for him somewhere out there. So he hopped a couple of buses and, a few days later, showed up unannounced at his kid brother's front door.

Not only did Roy welcome his big brother with open arms, he worked hard to help him clean up his act. And sure enough, after several months of sleeping on Roy's sofa, Ray began to improve. Thinking more clearly now, he started to realize how wrong he had been to just pick up and leave. So he made the decision to move back to Wichita and resurrect what, if anything, was left of his life. He really did miss Carol and his kids. So he took a bus home, still very apprehensive about how everyone would react to him. After all, he'd been gone for six months, and nobody really knew where he was.

When word got to Carol that Ray was back in town and staying with Gene, she drove the kids over so they could spend part of Thanksgiving with their father. But, afraid to see them, Ray asked Gene to tell them that it must have been a rumor that he was back in town. So they went away.

Early the next week, Ray went over to the corporate offices of Mr. D's Grocery Stores and asked for a job. Even though management was unhappy that he'd left in the first place, they fully realized that Ray Albert was a valuable asset, an extremely hard worker. All that was available at the moment, they told him, was a produce manager position at one of the stores. "I'll take it," he said quickly. "Thank you very much."

So Ray essentially started his career all over again—working at a level several rungs down from the position he had left only a few years before. And at times, it could be pretty mundane work: order the produce, unload it from the trucks, test it, place it on the shelves. But Ray viewed the routine as a form of therapy. Because the repetitive, rote nature of the job was stress-free, it allowed him to smooth out his roller coaster of emotions.

One day, during his third week on the job, Ray was checking the produce for imperfections. He pulled out some apples and bananas that had a few small spots on them. Still good enough to eat, they were not of the supreme quality required to be put on his shelves for sale. He then placed the fruit in a banana crate and was carrying it out to the loading dock when he happened to notice a couple of kids milling around the pile of empty boxes at the back of the store.

"Hey, kids!" he called out. "What's going on?"

The children reacted defensively, as if they had been caught doing something wrong. But Ray calmly reassured them. "No, no, it's all right," he said. "Come on over. I've got some extra apples and bananas here. Would you like them?"

As the kids each took a piece of fruit, Ray's mind drifted back many years to the day he had been searching for bananas with his brothers and sisters at the back of the Safeway store. It was back when they were all a family, back before they had been taken away and put in the orphanage.

"You all take care, now," he said to the children as they left.

"Merry Christmas, Mister," replied one of the boys.

Later that same evening, the doorbell rang at Carol Albert's house. Melinda and Scott were home alone because their mother had gone out shopping. When Scott opened the door, he saw a man with a beard standing at his door.

"Yes?" said the nine-year-old, clearly not recognizing who he was looking at.

"Scott, it's me, your dad," said Ray quietly. "I'm back."

Chapter Thirty-Nine

Knock. Knock. Knock.
Knock. Knock. Knock.
Knock. Knock. Knock.

"Yeah, Yeah, Yeah," yelled Ray from inside his small one-bedroom apartment. "Keep your shirt on. I'm coming. I'm coming."

Knock. Knock. Knock.

"Jesus, who the hell could be coming here this late at night?" he thought to himself as he rustled himself out of bed and slipped on his trousers.

Knock. Knock. Knock.

Ray removed the chain from the safety latch, opened the door, and found his sister standing there with two suitcases by her side.

"Norma Jean! What are you doing here?

"I tried Darlene, but she wasn't home. I was beginning to think you weren't here either."

"Well, Darlene never answers her door. What's going on?"

"I'm moving back to Wichita. Couldn't take Dayton anymore. Can I stay with you for a few weeks, just until I get situated?"

After Ray found this particular apartment, he'd sent Norma Jean a birthday card with his new address. On the card, he had written: "If you ever need anything, just let me know." And now, two weeks later, there she was, on his front doorstep—taking him up on the offer. What else could he do?

"Well, sure, I guess," he responded. "But this is a small place. You'll have to sleep on the couch."

"The couch will be fine."

The next morning, before Ray went to work, he gave Norma Jean a key and told her to make herself at home.

"Thanks, Raymond, I will," she said. "And I'll start looking for a job today. It'll just be a few weeks."

But Norma Jean never did find a job. In fact, she never even went on an interview. She just stayed around the house all day and went out drinking at night—sometimes coming home drunk, sometimes not coming home at all. And the "few weeks" she intended to stay turned into six weeks, then six months, then eight months. After about a year, she finally moved out of Ray's apartment and in with a guy she'd met at one of the downtown bars.

A few months later, Ray moved into a large three bedroom apartment with his brothers, Gene and Donald. All three men were single, it helped them save money, and it was better than living alone.

On moving day, after all furniture and boxes had been carried into the apartment, Gene brought out three beers and the brothers sat down and had a drink together. "Tell me, Ray," said Donald at one point, "how was it living with Norma Jean? How is she, anyway?"

"Hell, all she did was lay around on the couch all day and moan. And she'd never talk to me, never say a word. One time I got angry and ripped into her. 'Listen here, Norma Jean,' I said, 'I don't care if you swear or scream and yell, just talk. That's all I'm asking. Just talk.'"

"What did she say?"

"Well, she was apparently pretty drunk because when she rolled over, I could smell booze on her breath. Then she said, 'Leave me alone, goddammit. I'm divorced. I can't have children. I got no job, no life, nothing. And I don't need you giving me a bunch of grief. Just leave me alone.'"

"Jesus, that's awful!" said Donald.

"I'm telling you, she was stone cold drunk. When I moved the couch to bring it over here, I found a dozen empty whiskey bottles underneath."

"We have to help her."

"But what can we do?" asked Gene.

"Well, I don't know, but I'm gonna find out."

Donald knew about Norma Jean's history of drinking and mental illness, but he was completely unprepared for the way she lived her life. First of all, she refused to get a job. Second, she'd go out and pick up men at the local bars and go home with them. If they were amenable to taking care of her, she'd live with them. Donald also suspected that between men she was engaging in prostitution to make ends meet. And that really concerned him. So he began to spend more and more time with his sister— advising her, offering her a helping hand, giving her money every now and then. But the more time he spent with her, the more concerned he became. He learned very quickly that the men she became involved with were just as self-destructive as she was. Quite literally, they all seemed to be drinking themselves into oblivion.

Chapter Forty

Over the next five years, from the mid- to late-'70s, Norma Jean's life became a tragedy—despite the best efforts of her brothers to prevent it. She drifted from man to man, living with them, drinking with them, starving with them. Several times, Donald, Gene, and Ray had to take her in because the men in her life had thrown her out and left her homeless. Donald became her unofficial guardian—giving her money and helping her secure social aid. On her behalf, he applied for and secured both food stamps and general assistance from the state. He also got Norma Jean involved in Wichita's "Individual Assistance Program"—which was designed to help individuals stabilize their daily lives. Norma Jean's comprehensive plan included vocational rehabilitation, free bus transportation, a nutrition class, a sewing class, and an eventual move to low-income housing.

As much as Donald did for Norma Jean, nothing worked for very long and she continued a tragic downward spiral. Finally, in September 1976, she was hospitalized for a month in the mental ward of the Wesley Medical Center. Suffering hallucinations and delusions due to acute alcoholism and schizophrenia, she was treated with a variety of medications, including injections of Thorazine and Prolixin Decanoate—and pills of Valium, Dalmane, Cogentin, and Elavil. She also participated in group therapy and underwent a series of psychiatric examinations that resulted in her being placed on permanent medication to control her symptoms. And once again, she was warned to never touch another drop of alcohol.

After being released from the hospital, Norma Jean was provided ongoing State assistance and forced to live with twenty other people in a dilapidated halfway house in the low income section of Wichita. Showing signs of progress after three months, her formal psychiatric examination documented "considerable improvement in [her] condition and her psychotic symptomatology appears to be in good remission." In addition, the doctor's personal interview recorded that Norma Jean "denied experiencing hallucinations and delusions currently. She was oriented to her surroundings, and her memory, judgment, and concentration were grossly intact. She does have an adequate range of interests and her daily activities do not appear to be restricted."

Finally, in March 1978, Norma Jean was declared ready to leave the halfway house and go out on her own. Her official Kansas state medical report read as follows:

> The medical evidence indicates the claimant has the residual mental capacity to carry out the demands of competitive unskilled work. She may be unable to engage in her customary past work since the work required close conjunction with other people. However, at her age and with her educational background, she should be able to engage in sedentary low skilled work requiring tracking and hearing . . . Therefore, it is recommended that benefits be ceased effective 12/77.

Shortly after being released on her own recognizance, Norma Jean received a letter from the Wichita Department of Social and Rehabilitation Services stating that "your Medical Assistance case is being closed per your request" which meant, of course, that she wouldn't be receiving any more money from the state. Meanwhile, Gene and Dean (who were looking out for their sister now that Donald had taken a new job out of town) received a letter from the Hospital Collection Service stating that Norma Jean had an unpaid balance of $2,432.94.

When Dean asked her why she had requested stoppage of her state aid, she replied: "Well, they told me that I didn't need it anymore."

"But Norma, you're not cured yet and you're still on heavy medication," he replied. "You only have $2.83 in your checking account and you don't have a job. Where are you going to get the money to pay this bill? What are you going to live on?"

Norma Jean did not answer her brother. She just looked down at the floor.

Dean and Gene then took over and secured a reinstatement of her state benefits. They also filed an application for federal Social Security disability payments, but were denied.

About a month later, Norma Jean married Darrel D. Harrod—a man she had met at the halfway house. It was obvious that she had entered into the marriage in order to have a husband to help pay her way. But Gene was extremely alarmed, because he knew that Darrel was just another drunk—a twenty-four-hour-a-day alcoholic. A couple of weeks after the marriage, Gene ran into Darrel on his way to work one morning. Sitting out on the curb in front of the post office, Darrel had a two-inch gash on his head that was bleeding profusely.

"Darrel, what happened to your head?" Gene asked. "Have you been drinking?"

"No, I haven't had a drink for a month," came the slurred reply.

But Gene knew better. So he immediately took Darrel to the hospital to have his head stitched up and then drove him home.

Within six months, Norma Jean was back in the mental ward at Wesley Medical Center. She had been taken there by ambulance after apparently having been so drunk for so long that she had forgotten to take her medicine. That, in turn, resulted in hallucinations and body convulsions. This time she was confined to a padded cell for a week and placed on even higher doses of medication. When her condition finally stabilized, she was moved to a semiprivate room where she again underwent six weeks of psychiatric examinations and group therapy.

Six weeks later, Norma was released from the hospital and immediately filed for and received a temporary restraining order against her husband by which he was "restrained and enjoined from molesting [her] in any manner." Shortly thereafter, a formal decree of divorce was granted. The brothers also saw to it that all her attorney's fees were paid for by the Legal Aid Society of Wichita.

Thereafter, Gene took over as Norma Jean's unofficial guardian. He saw her regularly, took her to the county hospital to pick up her medicine, and worked with her to obtain a formal hearing which resulted in approval for Social Security disability benefits. As a result, in August 1979, Norma received a check for $4,857 in back benefits and subsequent monthly payments of $314.40. Unfortunately, she just frittered all the money away—purchasing large amounts of alcohol or giving it to men in the halfway house where she lived.

Finally, Gene, Dean, and Ray were forced to take more decisive action so that their sister would not totally self-destruct. On February 5, 1980, Norma Jean Albert was formally declared "an incapacitated person" and Gene was appointed her official legal guardian. Now, by court order, he would control all her finances and make all decisions with regard to her future.

Norma Jean did not object to the arrangement. Within a few weeks, however, she began trying to manipulate her brother. On one Saturday afternoon, for instance, she showed up at Gene's house with two male friends from the halfway house. She wanted to drive to Dayton, Ohio, she said, to see her ex-husband, Jerry, and her other friends. It would be a little vacation. But she needed some money for the trip.

"I need $500, Gene," she said. "I've got to have it."

But her brother steadfastly refused. "I'll buy the tickets and put you on a bus, Norma," he responded. "But if I give you the money, you'll just blow it on booze. There's no way I'm giving you $500. No way."

Chapter Forty-One

"Darlene Francis Albert, do you take Thomas J. Groetken to be your lawful wedded husband, to have and to hold, to love and to cherish, for better, for worse, in sickness and in health, until death do you part?"

"I do."

"Thomas Joseph Groetken, do you take Darlene Francis Albert to be your lawful wedded wife, to have and to hold, to love and to cherish, for better, for worse, in sickness and in health, until death do you part?"

"I do."

"Then by the power vested in me by the Catholic church and the State of Oklahoma," proclaimed Father Marquis Flowers, "I now pronounce you husband and wife."

Darlene was thirty-two years old, Tom sixty. They had known each other for six years, lived together for five, and for the past three, he had proposed to her every month. She'd always either said no or laughed it off. But one recent Friday evening, Darlene surprised Tom by saying yes. And on Saturday, May 17, 1974, they drove down to Newkirk, Oklahoma, a little town just across the Kansas border, where they could be married with no waiting and no fuss. The brief service took place at Church of the Nazarene, the only Catholic church anywhere around. Only three other people were present—the presiding Catholic priest, his sister, Faith Flowers, and Mrs. Alma Long, a local resident. The two women served as witnesses to the ceremony and, accordingly, signed the marriage certificate. Afterwards, Tom and Darlene drove straight back to Wichita.

Life didn't change much for the two of them after marriage. They were already settled in at their small, two-bedroom apartment at 1030 North Market, #203; Tom went to work every weekday at the post office, while Darlene stayed home and kept house. And they cherished their pet dog (a Chihuahua named Tequila). For Darlene, it was really a marriage of convenience. She wasn't getting any younger and didn't want to live alone for the rest of her life. Besides, all said, Tom was a pretty decent guy, and with his salary and benefits from the government, he could provide for her comfortably. Tom was also a lot like Darlene. He valued his privacy, pretty much kept to himself, and he liked to go out at night and "party hearty"—which the two of them did nearly every weekend in the first few years of their marriage. Other than those weekend forays, however, they were, for the most part, homebodies—rarely venturing out and almost never associating with other members of the family.

There was one exception, however. While Darlene steadfastly refused to attend any local church services, she did make it a point to pick up her mother once a month and drive out to St. Mark's Catholic Church to visit the cemetery out back where her sister, Mary Ann, and brother, Lonnie Lee, were buried. It soothed Clara greatly to be able to place flowers on the graves, and Darlene felt great empathy for her mother having lost two children so young in life.

Over the years, she and Tom went to St. Mark's frequently enough to become fairly well acquainted with the parish priest there, Father Edward York. He was a handsome man. Kind and unassuming, he also hailed from Kansas City—a fact that interested Darlene greatly. "Tell me about Kansas City," Darlene would ask him. "I've always wanted to go there. Is it a nice place to live? Is it a good place to raise a family? Is the Catholic church much different there than it is here? Tell me about the Catholic church in Kansas City."

Father York was so glowing in descriptions of his hometown, and Tom wanted so much to please Darlene, that Tom suggested they go up there every now and then for short vacations. It was only a three-hour drive, he noted. So why not make the trip? To his surprise, Darlene did not make all the normal excuses for not going—as she did with just about every other trip he suggested. And so they traveled to Kansas City frequently—staying in motels, seeing the sights, taking in a Cardinals baseball game once in awhile. Darlene also liked Tom to drive her around town. She liked looking at the houses and the buildings around East 27th Street. She liked to drive by schools when all the kids were outside—not the elementary schools, the middle schools—where the twelve-, thirteen-, and fourteen-year-olds hung out. "Stop here," she'd ask him. "Let's watch the kids for awhile."

Tom never knew why she was so interested in the schools. And Darlene never told him—never gave him so much as a hint, except to say how nice it might be to have a child, a son, one day. But every now and then, she'd unexpectedly burst into tears, and Tom would reach out and try to console her—whereupon she would push him away just as quickly and say, "No, let's go back to Wichita. Let's go now."

Frustrated after one such trip, Tom asked his brother-in-law, Gene, to go out for a drink with him after work at the post office. Over a couple of beers, Tom related the story and concluded the conversation by saying that "Darlene has weird ways."

"Well," responded Gene, "she didn't exactly have the easiest childhood, you know."

"What?" asked Tom. "What was so tough about it?"

Gene then related the Albert family history, the whole sordid thing, from scraping for food out of garbage cans to the orphanage to all the foster homes. And Tom was shocked. He had no idea because Darlene had never said anything about it.

"My God," he said. "I can't believe she never told me. Come to think of it, you know, she never talks about the past at all. Whenever it comes up, she just grabs another bottle. I guess now I know why."

Chapter Forty-Two

"Where's the booze, kid?" asked Gene's uncle.

"There's no alcohol here," Gene replied, "and there's not going to be any dancing either. I don't want another riot like at Ray's wedding. Just want to open the gifts and have a nice quiet celebration with some punch and a little food."

Gene and his uncles were standing at the entrance to the reception room of St. Anthony's Catholic Church in Wichita. It was July 17, 1976 and Gene had just married Esther Sole in the chapel.

More than two hundred people showed up for the ceremony. All Gene's siblings were there: brothers Ray, Dean, Donald, Roy, and sister Norma Jean. Darlene and Tom came, but left early and did not attend the reception. Just about all the Martins showed up as well, including Clara and her parents, Stephen, and all the cousins and aunts. The one glaring absence was Gene's father, Joe Albert, who had recently been diagnosed with prostate cancer. He had been having a lot of ups and downs, and as it turned out, Gene's wedding day was one of his bad days. Also in attendance were many friends and coworkers from the Post Office, which pleased Gene very much. And of course, members of Esther's immediate family were there—her sister, brother-in-law, and parents. Their extended family, however, was still back in Barcelona, Spain, from where they had emigrated in 1969.

A mutual friend had introduced Gene to Esther at a Catholic singles gathering right there at St. Anthony's Church. Now, three years later, at the age of thirty-two, Gene was a married man—something that he never thought he would become. For some reason, he had always been kind of pessimistic about his chances of finding the right woman. But Esther had changed all that, and he had been counting his blessings since the day he met her.

After opening all the presents and thanking everyone, the couple went over to her parents house to have several glasses of champagne. They were joined by Gene's twin brother Dean and Dean's wife and three children. Dean, it turned out, had gotten married back in 1970 when his girlfriend, Wilma, unexpectedly announced that she was pregnant. To avoid the three-day Kansas waiting period, they drove down to Newkirk, Oklahoma, for a quick shotgun wedding. The ceremony took place at the same Catholic church where Darlene and Tom would be married four years later. Dean now had three children, another was on the way, and he was as happy as he'd ever been in his life. He was also particularly excited and pleased for Gene—always the quiet and shy Albert brother—to have finally found someone with whom he could share his life.

After several toasts and a brief period of visiting, Gene and Esther headed off to Estes Park, Colorado, for a ten-day honeymoon. They got the idea to go there from Ray, who said he had visited Rocky Mountain National Park when he and Carol were on their honeymoon. Gene thought it a great idea—the perfect ending to a perfect plan.

Everything also seemed to be wonderful after they returned to Wichita. Gene received a promotion at the post office, he was getting along well with his new in-laws, and Esther was having a good time getting to know all of Gene's relatives. All except Darlene, that is, because about three weeks after the wedding, Darlene had called Esther and made a wild accusation.

"You know, of course, that Gene is running around with several other women, don't you?" she said.

"Darlene, that can't be true," Esther responded.

"Oh yes it is. I've seen him out at the bars at night with them."

"But he hardly ever goes out. He's here almost every night with me."

"Well, then, he must sneak out after you go to sleep."

"Don't be ridiculous, Darlene. That's absurd."

"Don't you talk to me like that, you little witch," screamed Darlene back into the phone. "If you aren't smart enough to believe the truth, then you deserve what you get. The hell with you."

That night, an understandably upset Esther told her husband about the phone call. "I'm pretty sure she was drunk, Gene. She was slurring her words, screaming and swearing. It was awful. Why would she do that?"

"I'm sorry that happened, Esther," he replied. "You didn't do anything wrong. Neither did I. Darlene's got some real emotional problems; she's had them for years. We've got to take these things in stride."

But the next morning, Gene called Darlene from work and asked her why she'd told Esther he was running around.

"Because you've been stealing my mail, that's why."

"No, Darlene, I have not. I don't even work in an area where that would be possible."

"Don't you lie to me, Gene. I know the truth. Some of my checks have been disappearing and you've been taking them. I know! I know!"

"Darlene, I wouldn't take any of your money. I wouldn't do that. You're wrong."

"Damn you, Gene," Darlene screamed and then slammed the phone down.

That same week, Donald Albert heard that his father had been diagnosed with prostate cancer and decided to fly to Wichita for a short visit. Remarkably, Joe drove himself to the airport to pick up his son.

"Jesus, Dad," exclaimed Donald. "What are you doing here? You shouldn't be driving."

"I'm fine, son. Get in. We're going over to pick up Darlene at the Pirate's Cave downtown before we head home. She wanted to see you. For some reason, she's always liked you the best of all you brothers."

"Okay, but why don't you let me drive."

"Just get in, boy," ordered Joe. "I'm fine."

When they arrived downtown, Donald went inside the bar to get his sister while his father waited in the car. He spotted her over in a corner drinking a beer by herself and when he called her name she wheeled and fell over onto the floor. Obviously drunk, Darlene called out to her brother and he went over and helped her up.

"Darlene, are you all right?"

"Yeah, I'm fine," she slurred back.

"Well, Dad is out in the car so we'd better go. Is Tom here?"

"Oh that bastard! He's always behind me."

"What do you mean he's always behind you?" asked Donald.

"You know, he's always wanting me to go out and make money for him at the bars. I don't want to tonight. I want to see you."

Donald didn't want to think about what that last statement might have meant so he just grabbed Darlene and led her outside to the car. After helping her into the backseat, he climbed up front with his father. On the drive over to Joe's place, Darlene began to chatter away. But much of what she said was unintelligible as she either mumbled or slurred her words. Suddenly, though, she began to sob hysterically and uncontrollably. Then she leaned forward, grabbed her brother's shoulder, and started screaming.

"I've had a baby!" she yelled. "I've had a baby! By a priest! By a priest!"

Donald was certain that his father heard what Darlene had just said. But Joe did not say a word. He just stared straight ahead and kept on driving.

Chapter Forty-Three

In his own way, Joe Albert had tried to build a relationship with his sons and daughters over the years. He would invite all of them over to his house to have Christmas dinner with him and his second wife, Gladys. And often, he would invite them over one at a time or in pairs. But, oddly, when they arrived, he would hardly say a word. Rather, he would just listen and smile. Sometimes he would simply stare up at the ceiling or down at the floor. It was his silence that everybody remembered. Joe Albert was quiet and tough, they said—quiet and tough.

And that's just the way he died in August, 1976, when prostate cancer finally got the best of him. "He never said a word on his deathbed," remembered Ray, who was with him at the end. "He just went completely silent—not a whisper or a moan, nothing. He just went silent."

Gladys immediately requested a full Catholic mass with burial at St. Mark's Church, and at first, the Wichita diocese approved the request. Ray and Donald also received verbal assurances that it would no problem. But the long arm of the Martin family (or perhaps their deep pockets) reached out again to cause some problems.

Even though a few cousins had mentioned to the Albert brothers that they didn't believe everything that happened to the family was all their father's fault, most of the Martins remained hostile toward Joe, even in death. And without a lot of fanfare, they let the powers that be know that Joe was a divorced man and, therefore, was not entitled to a formal Catholic funeral. The Martins also made it clear that their ongoing generous contributions to the Wichita diocese would be in serious jeopardy if such an exception was made in the case of Joe Albert.

On the day of the funeral, Ray was astounded to see the entire Martin side of the family there along with all the Alberts. The place was packed with more than two hundred people—many of whom filed past Joe's open casket as they walked in. But the presiding Catholic priest surprised Gladys and all the Alberts by not performing a mass. He just stood up front, said a few "Our Fathers" and "Hail Marys," and that was it. As a matter of fact, Joe Albert's name was not mentioned even once.

After about five minutes, the Albert brothers were instructed to pick up the casket and carry it out back for burial. A six-foot grave had been dug right next to little Lonnie Lee Albert. And Ray couldn't help but remember back some twenty-seven years, back to the time when he and his father had dug Lonnie Lee's shallow four-foot grave and watched as the small wooden pauper's casket was lowered into the hole. Now, he was standing in the same place—at his own father's burial.

And as the casket was slowly lowered into the grave, Ray heard his uncle Stephen mutter: "Now he's in hell where he belongs."

By contrast, when Clara Albert died two years later of complications from a stroke, she received a full Catholic funeral mass sanctioned and performed by the Catholic Diocese of Wichita. Two priests officiated and gave long, eloquent eulogies. Several members of the Martin family also got up and said many nice things about her. Ray was particularly upset at the death of his mother. Over the past several years, he'd made it a point to visit her regularly. Nearly every week, he would go out to the farm, and often she'd ask him to take her to the grocery store. Once there, she would pick up a bottle of Mogen David wine, some cherry pies, ice cream, and cookies—all the things her brothers wouldn't let her buy when they took her to the store. And then mother and son would go back to the little farmhouse and visit. Clara would sit in her rocking chair and look out the big living room picture window. Ray would sit next to her and they'd talk—about whatever was going on, about the harvest, recent visitors, the weather, her grandchildren.

Ray was also with his mother at the end. After the stroke, she'd lingered on for a couple of weeks—and he was there every day to visit her, often taking along his fifteen-year-old son, Scott. He even spent her last few nights at the hospital, sleeping down the hall in the waiting room, because he didn't want his mother to die alone. And while there, he often thought of all the times he had wanted to help her but could not make a difference in her life.

Clara Albert's waning years were tough. Never remarrying, she lived simply out on the farm with her brothers Alphonse and Stephen. Other than taking care of them, all she had to do was think about her life—and it tormented her.

She remembered her strict upbringing in the Catholic church. She was supposed to get married, have lots of kids, and raise them to be good Catholics. That was the secret to lasting salvation. So she ran off and married Joe Albert over the strenuous objections of her parents and brothers. Then she had trouble getting pregnant and wondered if she'd ever be able to have a child.

But children she did have—nine of them. And she tried to raise them well. She worked hard, oh so hard. But they came too fast and she couldn't keep up. Joe couldn't bring in enough money and there wasn't enough milk. That's why her baby, Lonnie Lee, died. She couldn't give him milk every day, because there just wasn't enough to go around. Mary Ann died because they didn't have enough money to get adequate medical care when she contracted rheumatic fever, which led to the heart condition that killed her. And Mary Ann died in a hospital all by herself—all by herself! My God, what kind of a mother was she? What kind of a mother? The hardest thing in her life was to have those two children die, she told Ray. It was the hardest thing.

And then there was the bond between mother and child. Clara had spent all those early years with her children only to have them ripped away from her—either by death, by the government, or by the Catholic church. Then she was thrown in jail and called an incompetent, bad mother. To top it all off, her family had her committed to the State mental asylum. She was diagnosed paranoid and schizophrenic, but in the remaining years of her life, she was mostly docile and quiet—left alone with memories and thoughts of her life. And thinking about all that day in and day out was almost too much for her to bear.

Clara Albert died a broken, mentally ill, unhappy, lonely woman. She was buried in the cemetery at St. Mark's Catholic Church next to Lonnie Lee and Mary Ann—reunited with her two babies at last.

Chapter Forty-Four

In mid-1981, Darlene's husband Tom was diagnosed with a cancer that started in his lower back and eventually spread through the rest of his body. When she found out the bad news, Darlene decided not to tell anyone in the family. But during the later stages of the illness, Gene heard about it from a friend at work and visited his brother-in-law in the hospital nearly every day. Unfortunately, on May 22, 1982, Tom Groetken died. Honoring his wishes, Darlene had him buried next to his first wife, Nell, at the Catholic Calvary Cemetery in Wichita.

Darlene received a significant life insurance payment and, combined with Tom's retirement benefits, she could have traveled and seen the world. Instead, she chose to live the life of a recluse—always keeping the shades pulled and almost never venturing out of her apartment, except to shop or go to a bar once in awhile. On the rare occasions when she did go out, she avoided speaking to anyone else if she could possibly help it. And for the rest of her life, she dressed only in black.

Every now and then, in an effort to keep in contact with his sister, Ray would go over to Darlene's apartment at North Market Street and knock on the door, but she would never answer. Same old thing, he thought. Darlene was secluded and still drinking heavily. He'd always wanted to help her. But Ray finally just stopped going over there.

In 1983, Ray's son Scott (then eighteen) had been living with his mother when she accepted a job in Dallas. But because he wanted to attend a local college, he made the decision to move into his own apartment. Scott was in his new place for several months before Ray realized it was the same apartment complex where his sister lived.

"Hey Scott, did you know that your aunt Darlene lives in apartment #203? How close is that to you?"

"Well, it's right next door," he replied incredulously.

"And you didn't know?"

"No. I've never seen anyone either coming or going from that apartment."

The next day, Scott knocked on Darlene's door, but she did not answer. He tried several other times that week all with the same result. A month or so later, Ray happened to run into Darlene at the grocery store and mentioned that her nephew lived next door to her.

"I know," she said casually, "I've seen him down by the pool."

Scott stayed in that apartment for about a year and never did see Darlene—not one time. But, then again, neither did anybody else who lived near her. She just stayed inside all the time.

By 1985, Darlene began to have some serious health problems. Nearly forty-four years old now, she had gained a great deal of weight—nearly one hundred pounds in the three years since Tom's death. She also experienced fainting spells, suffered from periods of intense, rapid breathing, and had developed a chronic hacking cough. In the spring, she finally broke down and went to see a doctor. After a complete physical, the doctor reviewed his findings with her.

"Mrs. Groetken, you've got problems with your liver, your kidneys, your lungs, and your heart," he informed her. "You must stop drinking, lose weight, and get some exercise."

"And if I don't?" she asked.

"Well, then, your body will simply give out. It's only a matter of time."

When Darlene heard that prognosis, her thoughts turned to the son she had given up for adoption some twenty-three years earlier. And she began to wonder how he had turned out, if he had gone to college, where he was living, if he was happy. These were all things she'd wondered about before, but now there was a sense of urgency to obtaining some answers. If she didn't take the time to find out, and do it now, she would probably never know.

So on June 2, Darlene wrote a letter to the St. Anthony's Home for Children in Kansas City. It read as follows:

Dear Sister,
    I would like information of my boy's adoption. He was born on February 7, 1962. He would now be 23 years old. I am a widow of 43 and never had other children. My husband of 18 years died of cancer. My last name was Wheeler. Sister Mathilde was there then. My doctor was Moriana. I left on February 20, 1962. Tell the girls hello and the sisters. You all are in my prayers.
Always,
Janet

Even though Darlene wrote her real name and address on the envelope, she did not get a response. So after six weeks had passed, she placed a telephone call to St. Anthony's to ask if they had received her letter.

"Yes, Mrs. Groetken," responded a nun on the other end of the line, "but we keep no files on the premises so we forwarded your letter to the Catholic Charities here in Kansas City. They performed all the adoptions in the 1950s and 1960s and surely will have any related material."

"Well, I haven't heard anything from them."

"I imagine these things take a little time."

"Is there a name you could give me?" asked Darlene. "You know, someone I could write to?"

"Yes, of course," she replied. "You might write to the associate director. The address is 1112 Broadway, Kansas City, Missouri 64105. If you wish to call him, his number is (816) 221-4377."

Darlene quickly placed a call to the associate director, but he was not available to speak to her. However, a secretary informed her that they had, indeed, received her letter and wondered if she had any more material they could go on. Did she, for example, have a birth certificate or any other vital information that might help make the search easier? Darlene replied that she did not but would try to obtain a birth certificate.

Within a few days, she mailed a check for eight dollars to the Bureau of Vital Records in Jefferson City, Missouri, and requested a certified copy of the birth certificate for her son, Bill Patrick Albert. A short time later, a return letter stated that "we made a search of the files and we are unable to locate a birth record in the name of [your son] born February 7, 1962. You state in your letter that the child was adopted, therefore, the birth record would be filed under the adopted name. Since the child has been adopted you are no longer a parent of record and we are prohibited by law from issuing you a copy of the birth record if located in the files."

Surely, the people at the Catholic Charities would have known that already, Darlene thought to herself. Why would they ask her to go get a birth certificate?

Oddly enough, that same week she received a note dated April 25, 1986 from a social worker. It stated that "her son" was a "healthy, well-adjusted adult" who had recently been married.

Well, at least now she knew that the Catholic Charities had located the records of her boy's adoption. But why hadn't they sent her the files or given her his name and address? Now Darlene's curiosity was piqued. Now she wanted to know everything.

Chapter Forty-Five

After many months of trading letters and phone calls back and forth with the Catholic Charities of Kansas City, Darlene finally received a call from the associate director, who let her know that he wasn't going to give her any more information.

"We can really be of no help to you, Mrs. Groetken, other than what we've already told you," he said. "We cannot breach the confidentiality agreement. And according to your own signed agreement, you cannot breach it, either—nor are you allowed to contact your son."

"Well, why didn't you tell me this before? Why did you give me all this runaround?"

"I'm sorry, Mrs. Groetken, but our hands are tied by the laws of the State of Missouri. We cannot legally provide you with the information you request."

"Well, I guess I'm going to have to go get a lawyer and sue you then!"

"Now, now, Mrs. Groetken, you don't want to do that. Maybe there's something else we can do. Tell you what. I'll send a request to the local judge and ask him to review the request and see what can be done."

"Well, I guess that'll be all right. When will you do that?"

"I'll do it right away and then send you a copy of my letter to him, okay?"

"Very well," replied Darlene. "I'll wait to hear from you."

Two weeks later, Darlene received a copy of the associate director's letter to Judge Donald Mason of the Jackson County Juvenile Court in Kansas City. "Attached is correspondence and case material from an adoption which occurred in Jackson

County," the letter read. "The relinquishing parent wishes to contact her son."

"Okay, now we're getting somewhere," thought Darlene.

But her optimism was short-lived because, on February 25, 1987, she received another letter from the associate director that essentially put everything back to square one. The Catholic Charities stated that the Jackson County Juvenile Court could not locate any records of her case—and they requested that Darlene tell them in which county the adoption was ordered and that she also send along any legal documents in her possession.

"But they have the records," Darlene screamed out loud. "They already told me they have the records. In fact, they sent them to the judge. 'The records regarding the placement of your son indicate.'—that's what the last letter said. They know what county the adoption took place in! What the hell's going on here?"

Darlene then wrote another angry letter of complaint. She also placed a call to the associate director but, as before, he was not available to speak to her. Finally, on March 13, 1987, Darlene received her final correspondence regarding the matter. This time it was from Judge Donald L. Mason of Jackson County, Missouri, who, in no uncertain terms, informed her that "nothing was found" in relation to the adoption of a William Patrick Albert. He also informed her that the adoption in question "took place in another county" and that he had no authority to release any information on the matter.

This time Darlene just threw the letter to the floor and began crying. "But they already knew which county it was," she said. "It was in the original records. What happened? Did they destroy the records or were they just lying to me?"

Darlene very meticulously folded this letter and placed it in the back of her newly purchased, cream-colored photo album with the other correspondence. It was only since Tom's death that she'd begun to collect and organize all her photographs and memories. This was her family album, her life's history which included her mother and father, her brothers and sisters, the orphanage, her days as May Crowning Queen, high school, St. Anthony's Infant Home, Tom Groetken, her drinking buddies, as well as what she considered her ultimate family, the Catholic church, and, of course, Father Daniel Mulvihill and the child they had conceived together. At the top of the first page, she placed her favorite picture of him along with the photo she had taken at her wedding with Tom. In between them, she placed the picture of a four-year-old boy named Allen she had cut out of TV Guide. He reminded her of Mulvihill—who should have been her husband. That's why she chose her wedding picture to place there. Darlene had obviously worked on her album for hours on end. But she never shared it with another living human being.

After receiving her most recent letter from the Jackson County, Missouri, judge, Darlene walked over to the bus station and purchased a ticket to Kansas City. On the way back home, she stopped by a liquor store and bought a bottle of bourbon and a bottle of champagne. She was going to go to Kansas City and find her son once and for all. And when she found him, she was going to invite him and his wife over for dinner and they were going to celebrate. It would be bourbon for cocktails and champagne after dinner. That was the plan.

Darlene made the trip to Kansas City on March 15, 1987. She stayed for several days and made the rounds—but came up empty. No one would help her. The nuns at St. Anthony's told her they had no information. The people at the Catholic Charities refused to acknowledge they had any files and, even if they did, they would be prohibited by law from letting her see them. And the judge would not make himself available to speak with her.

Finally realizing there was nothing else she could do in Kansas City, Darlene took a cab over to the local bus station. On the way, she had the cabby drive by St. Anthony's Infant Home.

"Just pull over here on the corner for a moment, will you, please," she asked when they got there.

One last time, Darlene gazed at the building. She peered around the side and saw the little playground where the toddlers used to play. And, for a moment, she envisioned a smiling little boy running into the arms of a nun. But her daydream suddenly evaporated when she realized there were no children anywhere around.

"Okay, let's go," she told the cab driver.

Then Darlene went to the bus station, bought a ticket, and rode home alone to Wichita.

Chapter Forty-Six

On the morning of July 25, 1987, Darlene rose at 6:00 AM to take her regular morning walk. Recently, she'd been having trouble breathing and finally decided to heed her doctor's advice about getting more exercise. Early mornings were best for her because that way she could avoid people. When she stepped outside, the sun was coming up low on the horizon and the birds were chirping. All in all, it was a beautiful, crisp, summer morning.

But Darlene only made it two houses down from her apartment building before collapsing to the sidewalk. Unable to catch her breath, and perspiring profusely, she managed to crawl to the steps of a house before losing consciousness. A passerby rushed over to her, then knocked on the door of the house and called an ambulance. Twenty minutes later, at Wesley Hospital (the same place her little sister Mary Ann had died thirty-eight years earlier), Darlene was pronounced dead. The cause of death was listed as "acute pulmonary edema" and "cardiac arrythmia." In other words, her lungs had filled up with fluid, and she'd suffered a massive heart attack.

Darlene Albert Groetken was only forty-five years old.

Later that morning, Gene received a call at work informing him of his sister's death. As next of kin, he was asked to come down to the mortuary to identify the body. He had not seen Darlene in a year or two and was barely able to confirm her identity. Gene was shocked by her huge weight gain and the nearly complete graying of her hair. It made her look like a woman in her seventies.

Gene immediately called his brothers and sister to give them the bad news. Roy and Donald flew into town right away and, the next day, they all gathered at Darlene's apartment to discuss funeral arrangements. As Ray was milling around the apartment, he noticed a manila folder resting on a kitchen shelf next to a small framed picture of Father Daniel Mulvihill. He picked it up and began thumbing through the papers inside.

"Look here," he announced. "Darlene purchased a vault in the Mausoleum at the Calvary Cemetery."

"What?" asked Roy. "Isn't that where all the bishops and priests are buried?"

"Yeah, I think so."

"But we already have family plots paid for at St. Mark's!" said Gene.

"Well, I know, but it doesn't look like Darlene wanted to be buried at St. Mark's with the rest of the family."

"Well, Calvary Cemetery is where Tom is buried, remember."

Dean then came over and took a look at the folder himself. "Look, here's a "Certificate of Right of Entombment" dated November 8, 1986."

"Why that's just nine months ago," noted Donald. "Do you think she knew she was dying?"

"It's signed by Rev. Vincent J. Eck, director of the Calvary Mausoleum."

"Looks official to me," said Roy.

"And here's a canceled check for $2,100.20 made out to Calvary Cemetery and signed by Darlene."

"Wait a minute," interrupted Roy. "Didn't you say she bought a vault in the mausoleum? Isn't Tom buried out back in the ground?"

"Yeah, that's odd. But clearly, she purchased this vault and not the plot next to Tom."

"Well, I guess that's it, then," said Ray. "We bury Darlene at the Catholic cemetery—in the mausoleum."

"Jesus, that's a lot of money to spend on a crypt," noted Gene.

"Well, I guess that's what she wanted. So let's make the arrangements."

Darlene's funeral was held at Resurrection Church, 4500 North Woodlawn, the parish Dean and his family attended.

Actually, Dean was the only family member who attended church at all—so Ray asked him if he would help with the arrangements.

The resident priest conducted a full Catholic funeral mass and said some very nice words about Darlene, but no one else spoke. And the casket was not open for viewing. About twenty-five people in all attended—mostly members from the Albert and Martin families. But a few of Darlene's old drinking buddies also showed up.

Following the mass, everybody went straight from the church to the Calvary Mausoleum. As the family gathered around, Darlene's casket was lifted up about fifteen feet and placed into the vault. At this point, Norma Jean began to get the shakes, but Donald wrapped his arm around her shoulders and held her hand to help steady her. Before the vault was closed and blessed, the priest read two brief prayers that Ray had found next to one of Darlene's small statuettes of the Virgin Mary.

> *We turn to you for protection,*
> *holy Mother of God.*
> *Listen to our prayers*
> *and help us in our needs.*
> *Save us from every danger,*
> *glorious and blessed Virgin.*

O MARY, conceived without sin, pray for us who have recourse to thee.
HOLY MARY, pray for us!
IMMACULATE HEART of Mary, pray for us now and at the hour of our death.
SWEET HEART of Mary, be my salvation!
OUR LADY, Queen of Peace, pray for us!

After the funeral, Ray, Dean, Gene, Donald, Roy, and Norma Jean went over to Darlene's apartment and boxed up all her belongings. They loaded nearly everything in apple boxes as fast as they could, not spending a lot of time looking at the things they were packing. The plan was to place everything in storage and sort out the details later. For now, though, they felt it was important to simply vacate the apartment.

Eventually, Ray and Gene sold off Darlene's furniture and gave all her clothes to charity. They also went through many of the cartons and ended up throwing out most of the contents.

About ten boxes remained unopened, though, and Ray just took them home and stacked them in his closet. He figured he'd get to them some time in the future.

Chapter Forty-Seven

On a cold morning five years later, Ray discovered Darlene's photo album buried at the bottom of one of the boxes in the back of his closet. That night he and his brothers huddled over a few beers at Gene's kitchen table, and a flood of repressed memories came flowing back. As they flipped through the album, they talked about the fact that Darlene must have had an illegitimate child by Father Daniel Mulvihill and then revealed to each other for the first time that four of them had been the victims of sexual abuse while in the El Dorado Children's Home. Ray quickly ended the discussion, however, when it became apparent that the revelations were becoming too painful.

After a couple of months of silence, the Alberts began to talk on and off among themselves. Roy, the youngest of the group, spearheaded the effort to sort out all the details—spending the next six months gathering information and talking endlessly to each of his brothers on the telephone. Once he thought he had the story together, he suggested that they do two things. First, they should consult a lawyer about the law in matters like this. Second, they should contact the Wichita Catholic diocese to see if any light could be shed on the subject.

"Surely the leaders of the church are unaware of all that happened," he said.

Roy traveled back and forth from San Francisco to Wichita several times in his search for legal advice. He consulted with a few California attorneys and several Kansas attorneys, but while some offered advice, none would formally represent his family. "It would be a real uphill battle," they told him.

After placing several calls to the Wichita diocese, Roy was finally directed to Rev. Ronald M. Gilmore, who in his position as vicar general was designated to act at the request of, and on behalf of, Bishop Eugene J. Gerber. According to church law, the position of vicar general in any diocese had to be occupied by a priest, at least thirty years of age, who was also "of sound doctrine, integrity, prudence, and possessing administrative experience." Rev. Gilmore seemed to fit all of those qualifications.

On July 14, 1994, at the Chancery Office of the Wichita diocese (424 North Broadway), Rev. Gilmore received Roy in a cordial and professional manner. He asked him to take a seat, moved behind his desk, and pulled out a pencil and pad of paper. Roy, who had brought Darlene's album and all the supporting paperwork, then began to relate the Albert family saga. He spoke about the circumstances that led the children to the orphanage in El Dorado, about Darlene's long-term relationship with Father Mulvihill, about her becoming pregnant with his child, and his driving her to Kansas City and checking her into St. Anthony's Infant Home.

After Roy paused to see if there was a reaction or questions, Rev. Gilmore simply said: "Well, thank you very much for coming in today."

"Wait a minute, Father," Roy replied, "that's not all of it."

"You mean, there's more?"

"Yes, a lot more."

Then Roy told him about Father Wheeler's molestations of himself, Donald, and Gene—with all the sordid details, including the physicals and the car trip to Boys Town in 1957. He also related the story about twelve-year-old Ray and his friend, Roger, who were taken advantage of by sisters Agnesina and Harrold.

For two hours, Gilmore listened attentively, asked a few questions, and took copious notes. "Now, don't you think it would be a good idea to have an investigation?" Roy asked the vicar general.

"Well, that's certainly a possibility," replied Father Gilmore. "Say, could you leave all this information with me—Darlene's album and everything in it?"

Roy immediately remembered the advice of one of the attorneys he had consulted: "Don't leave any originals with them, only copies," he had said. So Roy remained adamant with Gilmore.

"Father," he replied, "under no circumstances will I leave any of this original information with you or anybody associated with the church. You are not to be trusted. I will, however, be glad to provide you with copies, if you agree to conduct an investigation."

"Well, why don't you leave me a copy of the front page of Darlene's album and her graduation announcement where it mentioned she was going to become Father Mulvihill's special housekeeper."

"Okay," replied Roy.

"I understand that you have also been consulting with attorneys. Is that right?" asked Rev. Gilmore.

Surprised that the vicar general knew that they had been talking to attorneys, Roy simply replied: "Yes it is, Father. What do you expect when you find something out like this?"

"Well, can I get copies of your correspondence to them?"

"I don't see why not," Roy responded. "I don't have them with me, but I'll get them to you within a week."

"Very well, then."

Father Gilmore then stood up, walked around his desk, shook Roy's hand, and thanked him for coming in. And the last thing he said as Roy was walking out the door was:

"We'll investigate and, if this is true, we'll move heaven and earth to help your family."

Chapter Forty-Eight

Over the next several months, Rev. Gilmore gathered more information from the Albert brothers. In August, he met personally with Gene and, in September, spoke by telephone with Donald. Dean did not participate in the process—maintaining all the while that he was not abused in any way, nor did he have a quarrel with the Catholic church. Ray, however, did not participate for a completely different reason. He would not give Gilmore the time of day because he did not trust the Wichita diocese or anyone associated with it.

Ray had never gotten over the time the church tried to remove him from the Babcock's home to send him to an out-of-state reformatory. He also remembered how Sheriff Babcock had taken the church to court and won.

"They've always been on us—ever since we were little kids," he said to his brothers. "They want to control us, lead our lives for us, make us do what they want us to do. I've had it with the Catholic church and everything that goes with it. I want them off my back. I want them out of our lives.

"They only way we're going to resolve this thing is to do it through the courts," he said. "They will never, ever admit to anything. They will try to twist our words and make us sound like the bad guys. You just watch. I will not deal with them. And you are making a mistake by doing so."

Still, Roy, Donald, and Gene felt it was best to work through the process and at least try to give the church a chance to do the right thing.

When it was Gene's turn to speak with Rev. Gilmore, he was nervous and apprehensive about meeting one of the leaders of the church. Nevertheless, he spoke openly and in detail about his abuse at the hands of Father Wheeler and Sister Joachim. Just as in the meeting with Roy, Rev. Gilmore was cordial. He sat behind his desk, listened intently, took a lot of notes, and asked questions. In a little while, Gene's nervousness vanished—and the more he talked, the more angry he became at all that had happened. When the interview ended, he simply looked at Rev. Gilmore and shook his head in disgust.

"The Catholic church might do a lot of good, Father," said Gene, "but sexual abuse of children is *wrong!* It's just *wrong!*"

A period of about eight months passed before Rev. Gilmore would get back to the Albert brothers regarding his opinions and findings. During that interim period, Gene was contacted by an attorney's office operating in the eastern part of Wichita. They had heard about the Alberts' situation, they said, and were very interested in taking the case. If the Alberts wanted to sue the Catholic church for damages, it wouldn't cost them a thing. The case could be taken on a 40 percent contingency basis. The attorneys would only be compensated if they won. But before they could determine the merits of the case, the Alberts would have to let them review all supporting documentation. "We need to know what 'hard' evidence you have," the lead attorney said.

"At last, a law firm who's willing to work with us," thought Gene. So he decided to give this attorney copies of everything he had in his possession, including all Darlene's paperwork, some of the photo album pages, Darlene's receipts at St. Anthony's when she had the baby, and her correspondence to the Catholic Charities.

But several months later, the lead attorney wrote a letter to Gene saying he was no longer interested in taking the case. He offered no explanation as to why he had changed his mind and he returned all the material that had been provided. Curious as to why the sudden change of heart without any explanation, Gene started asking around town about this law firm. And it turned out that the attorney he had been speaking with came from a wealthy Catholic family and was a good friend and golfing partner of Bishop Gerber.

When Gene passed on this little bit of information, Roy simply shook his head in disbelief.

"Damn, Gene," he said. "We might have just been snookered."

Roy finally received a formal written response from the vicar general on April 20, 1995. The Rev. Ronald M. Gilmore began his four-page letter by stating that the Wichita diocese was prepared to pay for psychiatric evaluations for Roy, Gene, and Donald, and that, depending on the recommendations, they would discuss the possibility of ongoing therapy. Then he addressed "the claims you and your brothers have made."

With respect to Darlene, he stated that it was "beyond question" that she had a child out of wedlock and that, as a friend, Father Mulvihill did state he had driven her to Kansas City. However, he also reported that Mulvihill "flatly denies" that the child was his—and that there was nothing in this priest's background that would indicate anything of the kind happened—and that the scrapbook alone was ambiguous evidence. Therefore, said the vicar general, "the burden of proof remains on you."

He also wrote that they had interpreted the entire episode incorrectly. Rather, it could be interpreted as "the dreaming of a lonely young woman about a kind and handsome young priest" and "about what she wished could have been." There was simply no proof of what the brothers had alleged, and he was now considering Darlene's part in their story "a closed chapter."

With respect to the abuse alleged by Gene, Roy, and Donald, the vicar general stated that before Father Wheeler died, he "flatly denied" all the allegations—and that there was nothing in "Father Wheeler's file" or "in his history" that suggested he had "any such problem." The burden of proof, therefore, remained on the three brothers, and the entire episode was reduced to nothing more than their word against his. The vicar general's "legal advisors," he wrote, told him that "there is nothing here." But his "mental health advisors" told him that there was "some possibility to the story."

With respect to Ray's allegation, however, he totally dismissed the entire story because Sister Agnesina Metzinger was not at the orphanage until three years after Ray claimed she was—and that Sister Harrold was never there at all. Both women, he informed them, were now deceased. In addition, he said he had spoken with Ray's friend Roger, who told him the entire claim was not true and that he would be willing to "fly back to testify" if it were required. "I am thus left with nothing more than Raymond's word," he wrote—and that was not good enough.

After denying all the brothers' allegations, Rev. Gilmore then questioned their motives in bringing their story up in the first place. Why had they first gone to an attorney to explore "all their legal options"? he wondered. He also accused them of hinting that it would be terrible if the story ever got out, of hinting that they were going to the newspapers, and of hinting that they might write a book. He then related that in his experience, most people in their situation would first want professional therapy. "You reach for it in a most curious fashion," he wrote.

In closing, Reverend Gilmore stated that his "overriding concern" was with the truth. And then he vowed to them that if they had done something wrong, "we will move heaven and earth to make it right."

Chapter Forty-Nine

Roy faxed copies of Gilmore's letter to his brothers and, that night, organized a telephone conference call with Ray, Gene, and Donald to discuss its contents.

"Well, what do you guys think?"

"Jesus, is he accusing us of lying to get money?" asked Donald.

"Hell, we never hinted at anything like he's suggesting—going public, newspapers, a book," Roy replied. "He's suggesting that we're just in it for the money and he's trying to lay the blame right back on us. You were right all along, Ray."

"I don't know about you guys, but I feel like I'm being abused all over again," said Gene.

"Yeah, they literally degrade you and molest you again."

"And look at this. He says, 'My legal advisors tell me there's nothing here.' You know, he didn't really get enough information from us for a lawyer to make that kind of determination. He never asked for more copies of anything. I'll bet that guy who told us he wanted to take the case on a 40 percent contingency gave him all the information. He was probably a plant all along. When they got the information they wanted, he dropped us like a hot potato. Just strung us along the whole way."

"That son-of-a-bitch! He calls Darlene 'a lonely young woman' and Mulvihill a 'handsome young priest'—and then says we can't prove anything."

"This is diabolical!"

"Well, one thing's pretty obvious. These people aren't going to do anything. They don't care. We've got to go out and get an attorney, now."

"Yeah, let's sue the hell out of them."

"But who can we get? Nobody we talked to was willing to take the case."

"We'll find somebody if it takes ten years," vowed Roy.

About a week later, Roy was reading the local newspaper in his apartment in San Francisco when he came across an article about sexual abuse in the Catholic church. It seemed that the local diocese was having some problems with pedophile priests, and a number of people had come forward to state that they were molested as children.

In the article, the local bishop was quoted as saying: "If anybody out there has been molested, please come and see us." So Roy made a phone call and, on May 9, 1995, he went to the Chancery Office of the Catholic Archdiocese of San Francisco and met with Bishop McGrath and his assistant, Father Engle. Roy took all the supporting information and made the same presentation he'd given Gilmore in Wichita.

After listening for two hours, Bishop McGrath turned to Rev. Engle and said: "I've never seen this much documentation in a molestation case—ever."

Then Roy showed them Gilmore's letter of response. After reading it, the Bishop turned to Roy.

"Mr. Albert, we would have never responded to your family like this. And we certainly wouldn't have made such a degrading reference about your sister."

"Yeah, but aren't you all the same church?" asked Roy.

"They're a different diocese, we're a different diocese. But we would never have done that to your family."

"Well, can you help us?"

"Unfortunately, we are powerless to do anything for you. You have to go back to Kansas."

"Well, we have been in Kansas and look what Father Gilmore says."

"I'm sorry, Roy, we cannot deal with this."

With that, Bishop McGrath said goodbye and Father Engle escorted Roy to the door and showed him out.

Meanwhile, back in Kansas, the Wichita Catholic diocese announced that Father Daniel Mulvihill was temporarily leaving the state on an "educational sabbatical at the Center for Continuing Formation in Ministry." He was going to the University of Notre Dame in Indiana.

Chapter Fifty

Over the next two weeks, Ray organized all the paperwork and material—very carefully placing everything in chronological order so it could be easily understood by any lawyer who might take their case. He also conducted additional research by going through court archives and making copies of records related to the removal of him and his siblings from their parents' home and subsequent placement in the orphanage. And at one point, he boldly walked into the archives of the Catholic diocese and asked one of the nuns in charge for any information they might have regarding the St. Joseph Home for Children in El Dorado and the children who were sent there. Not knowing who Ray really was, the sister informed him that she'd had some recent requests for that material and couldn't find it. "It must have been lost or destroyed over the years," she said.

Further alarmed by Rev. Gilmore's assertion that Sister Agnesina Metzinger was not at the orphanage when he was there, Ray drove all the way to Dodge City, Kansas, to look up her history with the Catholic church. He had been told right after the incident that Sister Agnesina had been transferred to St. Mary's of the Plains and, sure enough, right there in the records it documented her arrival on September 5, 1952. The chronology further listed her as being at the St. Joseph Home for Children from 1955–1957 and then moving on to Oklahoma City's St. Anne Home for the Aged in 1957. There was, however, no reference to Sister Agnesina being in El Dorado earlier but, then again, she had told Ray that she had not yet taken her vows. Perhaps the record only reflected the "official" time she was a nun, he thought. Or perhaps the record was altered. After all, they did hustle her out of there with a cloud over her head. One thing was for sure, though, he and his brothers were certain that Sister Agnesina was not at the orphanage when the record stated she was. That would have meant she had been there when the place closed down—and there was simply no way that could be true.

Ray received another bit of shocking information when he discovered an article about the Metzinger family of Caldwell, Kansas. The eighth and youngest child, named Irene, later became a nun named Sister Agnesina, related the article. It listed the year of her birth as 1914—which meant that she had actually been thirty-eight years old in 1952, not nineteen as she had told Ray. "Jesus," he thought to himself. "That means she probably hadn't just taken her vows, either."

While Ray gathered and organized material, Roy and Gene embarked on an intensive search to find someone to take their case. After checking all around the Wichita area, one legal firm finally recommended a local attorney named Marlys Marshall. "She's the one you have to get," came the endorsement. "She handles these types of cases. As a matter of fact, she's working on a very similar case that is in front of the state supreme court right now. She's great and she really cares."

That was good enough for Roy and Gene, who immediately contacted Ms. Marshall and set up a meeting to tell her their story and review the material Ray had collected. After the presentation, she offered to take the case for a certain amount of up-front money, and then, if the lawsuit made it all the way to court, she'd work on a 40–45 percent contingency basis. Roy and Gene agreed to the arrangement, and their new attorney immediately set about writing the lawsuit.

Just prior to filing the action, Marlys asked for and was granted a meeting with Rev. Gilmore to discuss the details of the lawsuit and to find out whether or not they wanted to opt for some sort of settlement. Also present at the meeting was counsel for the Wichita diocese, Mr. Francis Hesse, who was the very same attorney who had handled part of the Albert case for the diocese in its early stages; he was also the same man Ray had met with more than twenty-five years before, when he was trying to get his mother out of the mental institution at Larned. At that time, Hesse had told Ray that he wasn't capable of taking care of Clara because she was too far gone.

The meeting with Rev. Gilmore and Mr. Hesse did not last more than a few minutes and, when it was over, Marlys immediately called Roy and Gene. "There's no way they're going to deal," she told them. "No way."

The Albert brothers then gave her the go-ahead to file the lawsuit, which she did on May 16, 1996, in the civil department of the Eighteenth Judicial District Court of Sedgwick County, Kansas. It named as defendants the Catholic Diocese of Wichita, Catholic Charities, and Rev. Daniel Mulvihill, "an individual currently residing at St. Rose of Lima Catholic parish at 115 W. Walnut, Columbus, KS 66725." The defendants were sued on ten counts, including: child sexual abuse; assault and battery; outrageous conduct causing severe emotional distress; invasion of privacy; negligence; negligent retention and supervision; breach of fiduciary relationship; fraud; fraud through silence; and civil conspiracy. Subsequent briefs detailed the entire saga:

> In 1949, Eugene, Donald, Raymond, Roy, Dean, Norma Jean, and Darlene Albert were minor children living in Sedgwick County, Kansas. The Albert children were taken into protective custody by the State of Kansas as children in need of care as a result of parental neglect. Thereafter, the Albert children were adjudicated wards of the State and were placed into the care, custody, dominion and control of the Catholic Church in Wichita, Kansas . . . The Church thus became the guardians of the Albert children.
>
> All of the Albert children were placed at St. Joseph's Home in El Dorado, Kansas, an orphanage owned, operated, managed and sustained by the Catholic Diocese of Wichita and St. Joseph's Home and their agents, representatives, servants, and employees . . . The Albert children were totally dependent upon and reliant upon the Church as their care givers for their survival and safety.
>
> All of the Albert family was violated and abused by various perpetrators while in the custody and control of the defendants. After the death of their sister, Darlene, the remaining Albert plaintiffs discovered the existence of an illegitimate child born to Darlene Albert as a result of her sexual abuse by one of the Catholic priests responsible for

her care: as a result of that revelation, the remaining family members became cognizant of the pervasive damage each had sustained as a result of the pernicious abuse perpetrated at the orphanage . . . Each child was subjected to multiple acts of severe sexual and physical abuse by multiple perpetrators.

Their sister had conceived and borne a child as a result of the unlawful and wrongful sexual acts of defendant Mulvihill during her minority and while she was still in the custody and control of the defendants.

The Alberts requested "reasonable damages in excess of $50,000, with costs incurred herein and such other and further relief as the Court deems just and proper." Hoping to avoid a politically controlled judge, they also asked for a jury trial.

As part of their evidence, the Albert brothers went on record by giving depositions in the form of written narratives. Along with providing the details of their stories, each included the following more personal comments:

Eugene A. Albert
The family received a reply from Fr. Ronald Gilmore on April 20, 1995. He is the Vicar-General to the Bishop, and his letter was shattering to the family. He denigrated the family and Darlene who suffered greatly during her life.

I thought the Catholic Church stands for truth, justice, and compassion. Our family has not received any of these, but we were exploited by them as children.

In closing, I would like to relate that what has happened to our family is a tragedy, but what has happened since receipt of Fr. Gilmore's letter is diabolical.

Roy L. Albert
These incidents have been buried in my mind, but since the deaths of my sisters, Darlene and Norma Jean, and the circumstances surrounding their deaths, these incidents have been brought back . . . All of these revelations have made me angry and quite upset. I do realize that I need some professional care to help me deal with these different situations.

Raymond L. Albert

At the age of 12, I spent two nights with Sister Agnesina. When all this came back, I went to St. Mary's looking for her. But they told me she had died on June 18, 1978. I felt her arms reaching for me, pulling me toward her. Part of me is with her. That evening driving home on the canal route, the van felt like going toward her.

If I had known what Father Wheeler did to my little brothers at the time, I would have killed him . . .

There is no amount of money I can put on what happened to our family.

Donald A. Albert

I hope justice will prevail, and that the priests and Catholic church will be held accountable.

On May 17, 1996, the day after the lawsuit was filed, a reporter from *The Wichita Eagle* called Bishop Eugene Gerber's office seeking official comment from the Catholic diocese. After being referred to Rev. Gilmore and conducting an interview, the reporter informed the vicar general that the story was slated to run on the twenty-first.

A local television station also decided to run a story on the lawsuit, and they sent a reporter and cameras out to both the diocese and the orphanage in El Dorado. That piece, too, the diocese was informed, would run on the twenty-first.

In the next issue of *The Catholic Advance,* the official newspaper of the Diocese of Wichita, the following announcement appeared:

> Rev. Daniel R. Mulvihill, formerly pastor of St. Rose of Lima, Columbus, and St. Bridget, Scammon, retired on May 19, 1996.

Chapter Fifty-One

On May 21, 1996, two days after Father Mulvihill was retired by the Catholic church, *The Wichita Eagle* made the Albert lawsuit public with a story headlined: "Siblings Contend They Were Abused at Children's Home." "Four brothers who say they were sexually abused in an El Dorado children's home 40 years ago have sued the Wichita Catholic Diocese," the first paragraph read.

After relating the basic facts and details of the legal action, the article went on to report that "[Father Daniel] Mulvihill did not return phone calls seeking comment." Vicar general Ronald Gilmore, however, was quoted extensively. "We think the complaint is unfounded and we ought not to be involved in this lawsuit at all," he said. "We could find no real substance to their complaint." Gilmore also stated that he had "a responsibility to protect innocent people from unfounded legal action."

Marlys Marshall was quoted as saying that the Albert brothers had the right to sue the diocese "because they realized— albeit 40 years later—that the abuse they suffered caused them years of mental and physical pain and suffering." The article further pointed out that the Alberts "want the church to change the way it deals with abuse and to make sure any abuse that might be going on is stopped."

When Wichita's local NBC television affiliate, Channel 3 (KSN), ran their story later that same day, Rev. Gilmore remarked on camera that the diocese had conducted a two-year investigation into the charges and that, in the end, he was not convinced the Alberts suffered any abuse at all. "The charges of abuse seemed to be ambiguous to me," he said. "I know the family had a very difficult time and they've had a really tough life. But it seems to me that when they come right down to these specific, practical things they're alleging, they don't have the documentation to prove it . . . These things do happen. They have happened. Do they happen with any more regularity in the church than elsewhere? I don't think so."

The Alberts declined the offer to be interviewed on television. Off camera, however, Marlys stated that money was not the point of the lawsuit—that the brothers just "wanted the truth to be known so other children will not be in danger."

"Father Gilmore's response?" related the reporter: "He says false accusations can be equally dangerous."

Had the reporters from *The Wichita Eagle* and KSN News realized it at the time, they might have asked both Rev. Gilmore and Marlys Marshall about similarities between the Albert brothers' lawsuit and two others that had recently been adjudicated.

Another client of Marlys's had just lost a very similar case that was presided over by the same judge (D. Keith Anderson) who had been assigned to the Albert case. The first appeal had also been lost and the case was currently in front of the Kansas State Supreme Court.

On behalf of her client, Joleta Ripley (age fifty), Marlys filed a civil action against Ripley's father, B. E. "Jack" Tolbert, alleging that he sexually abused her when she was a minor. Pearl Tolbert, Ripley's mother, was also named for not preventing the sexual abuse. Ms. Ripley asserted that she had "spontaneously experienced a memory recall of her father sexually abusing her" approximately thirty years after the event.

In finding for the defendants, the lower courts cited two Kansas state laws that revolved around the statutes of limitations for such offenses. Regarding K.S.A. 60-523, the court quoted directly from the statute:

> No action for recovery of damages suffered as a result of childhood sexual abuse shall be commenced more than three years after the date the person attains 18 years of age or more than three years from the date the person discovers or reasonably should have discovered that the injury or illness was caused by childhood sexual abuse, whichever occurs later.

Similarly, the court pointed out that K.S.A. 60-515

triggered the eight-year statute of limitations for minors on the date of the negligent act. This language makes it clear that the 8-year statute of repose applies to all tortious acts committed while the plaintiff is a minor, regardless of how old the plaintiff is when the action actually accrues.

Undeterred at these losses in the lower courts, and backed by her client, Marlys proceeded to appeal *Ripley v. Tolbert* to the State Supreme Court for final judgment.

In the second related case, Marlys Marshall's law firm had also represented Wendell E. Gravley in a lawsuit against Rev. Robert D. Blanpied and the Catholic Diocese of Wichita that alleged the exact same ten counts as in the Albert case: childhood sexual abuse, assault and battery, outrageous conduct causing severe emotional distress, etc. Gravley, after thirty years of re-pressed memories, recalled being repeatedly sexually abused (when eleven years old) by Blanpied, a priest employed by the Catholic Diocese of Wichita. The suit alleged, among other things, that when the matter was brought to the attention of church leaders, Father Blanpied was transferred to another par-ish within the diocese and that in 1994, Blanpied, in the presence of Gravley and his family, "freely admitted his childhood sexual abuse of plaintiff."

During the first week in February 1996, a full three months prior to the filing of the Alberts' lawsuit, Gravley lost his case. Summary judgment was rendered in favor of the defendants, in part because the statute of limitations had run out and "action is time barred under both K.S.A. 60-523 and K.S.A. 60-515."

In essence, then, two very recent lawsuits similar to the one the Albert brothers filed had not fared well at all in the lower courts. The rulings were consistent and straightforward: Kansas law stated that a person cannot sue within three years of remem-bering a past abuse if the time between the abuse and the recol-lection was more than eight years. It was just that simple.

Subsequently, on August 14, 1996, three months after the Albert suit was filed, the Kansas State Supreme Court issued its final judgment against Ripley and for the defendants, Mr. and

Mrs. Tolbert. In support of their ruling, the Supreme Court justices cited the appropriate Kansas laws. "A statute of limitations extinguishes the right to prosecute an accrued cause of action after a period of time," the judgment read. "K.S.A. 60-515, which imposes an 8-year statute of repose for minors, does not violate the right to equal protection and due process of law."

Attorneys for the Catholic Diocese of Wichita seized upon the Supreme Court's ruling and, at the end of November, filed for a summary judgment on the Albert lawsuit. Presiding judge D. Keith Anderson wasted little time in issuing a ruling. Less than a week later, he cited *Ripley v. Tolbert* and decided that the statute of limitations had, indeed, expired. That ruling was filed on December 3, 1996—what would have been Darlene Albert's fifty-fifth birthday.

Defendants motion granted. Case dismissed.

Despite the ongoing series of defeats, Marlys Marshall simply would not give up. For her, it was more than a simple case of sexual abuse. It was a matter of principle. It was about right versus wrong. Something had to be done for the Alberts and people like them, she believed—and this Kansas statute simply had to be declared unconstitutional and thrown out. Her passion eventually persuaded Roy, Gene, Donald, and Ray to take the case the next step, to the Court of Appeals in Topeka.

In her appeals brief, filed on June 18, 1997, Marlys argued the case eloquently:

> No group of potential claimants is more deserving of civil rights protection than the class comprised of innocent children who have been physically tortured and emotionally incapacitated by their forced submission to criminal sexual child abuse, particularly those who lack anyone to advocate or protect them because their guardians are their perpetrators. Surely no class of Kansas citizens is so utterly blameless for the often lengthy lapse of time between the occurrences of child abuse and the much later date upon which such a victim may attain the perception, awareness, understanding, will, resolve, courage, and emotional capacity to comprehend and "ascertain" the childhood victimization and its consequent damage to his or her life.
>
> Moreover, no class of wrongdoer is less deserving . . . than the pedophile who . . . secretly rapes and violates a

child in a manner so physically and psychologically repugnant as to cause the victim's involuntary mental segregation of the event and subsequent ignorance of the harm in order to live through it.

For adult survivors of such devastating childhood trauma, the possibility that our laws could be so poorly conceived and realized, that they might be misinterpreted to unjustly immunize such a perpetrator from any measure of accountability for the injury and damage inflicted is yet another bitterly disappointing revelation.

Chapter Fifty-Two

Six months after the Albert's appeal was filed, in December 1997, a tall, handsome, thirty-five-year-old man walked into the Chancery of the Archdiocese of Kansas City, Missouri, and asked permission to conduct some research in the archives. He knew that he had been adopted through the Catholic church in Kansas City back in 1963, he said. He had been born on February 7, 1962, to an unwed young woman and then kept in some sort of orphanage until his adoption about a year later. He had a copy of the key legal paperwork and his parents had told him all they knew. But he wanted to know more, because he was starting a family and he thought it would be a good idea to obtain some medical background information on his biological parents. And he couldn't explain why, exactly, but he had recently been experiencing an abiding desire to contact his real mother.

"My name is T. J. Smith," he said. "Can you help me?"

"I'm sorry, Mr. Smith, but we don't have any of that information here," came the reply. "You'll have to work through the Catholic Charities over at 1112 Broadway. But they won't just let you look through their files yourself. I'd suggest you write a letter of inquiry to them."

T. J. followed the suggestion and initiated an exchange of written correspondence with the Catholic Charities. He supplied basic information surrounding his adoption and proof of his own and his parent's identities.

A number of months later, he received a call from a caseworker assigned to work on his request.

"Mr. Smith, we've determined that your birth mother is deceased. We know that her name was Darlene Albert Groetken and that she died in Wichita on July 25, 1987. We do not, however, have any other information on her at this time. Nor do we have any information on your birth father."

"Is that all you can tell me?" T. J. asked.

"At this time, yes it is. Would you like us to continue searching?"

"Yes, I would."

"Very well, Mr. Smith. We'll be happy to do so, but the Catholic Charities requires a fee of $250 to do the search you're requesting."

"Okay, I'll mail you a check tomorrow."

It would be another couple of months before T. J. would receive his second call from the caseworker.

"Hello, Mr. Smith. I just wanted to call and provide you with an update. I've been able to secure more information on your birth mother, but the information surrounding your birth father is very vague. As a matter of fact, it's really strange but that part of the file is missing. It's just not there."

"So what do we do now?" asked T. J.

"Well, I'll keep searching. There are a couple of other places I've yet to check."

"Can you send me what you have on my birth mother?"

"Well, actually, our policy is to complete the entire search and then provide you the information all at once. I hope that will be all right with you."

"Sure it will. I'll wait."

In June 1998, exactly one year after the Albert brothers had filed the appeal in their case, three judges on the Kansas Court of Appeals upheld the lower court's finding. Basically, they ruled that Kansas state laws applied and that the statute of limitations had simply run out.

The abuse the Alberts claimed had all happened too long ago, the court said. Therefore, it did not matter whether or not the Wichita Catholic diocese's actions, or Father Daniel Mulvihill's, or Father William A. Wheeler's could be proven or not. They could not legally be held accountable at this late date.

The next step for the Albert brothers was to take their case to the State Supreme Court. But in laying out the possibilities for success, Marlys was not optimistic. She cited the recent rulings in the *Ripley v. Tolbert* and *Gravley v. Blanpied* cases and told the brothers that the chances of a favorable outcome were not good. In addition, it would cost at least another $14,000 to be paid up front and they would have to get themselves another attorney. She was getting married and moving out of state.

When the brothers met privately to discuss the decision whether or not to move forward, Roy was the only one who really wanted to keep going.

"We've got to go all the way to the US Supreme Court with this, if necessary," he said. "We've got to raise awareness and make the Catholic church pay for what they did."

Donald and Gene were leaning against any further appeals. But before they could speak, their decisions were sealed when Ray spoke out in an emotional and decisive manner.

"No! I've had enough!" he said firmly. "I've had enough of the Catholic church! I've had enough of lawyers and the legal system! I've had enough of everything! I can't take it anymore. I just can't take it anymore. It's over."

Chapter Fifty-Three

Almost immediately after the final appeal was lost, Ray threw himself into his work. He hit the road for almost three months straight—traveling all over Kansas and Oklahoma, wherever his company sent him. He just did not want to think about the lawsuit, the church, or anything else.

But on August 25, 1998, he returned to his hotel in Baxter, Kansas, after spending all day setting up a convenience store. As he began looking through the telephone book to find the number of one of the store owners, he noticed a listing for Father Daniel Mulvihill at St. Patrick Church in the small town of Galena—located only eight miles away.

"What's this?" Ray thought to himself. "I wonder if he didn't really retire after all—if all that was just a smoke screen."

On impulse, he dialed the number and, after about four rings, a man answered.

"Is Father Mulvihill there?" asked Ray.

"No, he's not," came the response. "He lives in Joplin, Missouri, right now. Just moved there not long ago."

"Well, can you tell me what church he's affiliated with, please?"

"He is no longer the pastor of a church. He retired because of a paternity suit. Right now, he's in Ireland on a vacation."

"Huh? A paternity suit, you say? Well, okay, thank you."

Ray just hung up the phone and shook his head in amazement.

"Darlene's dead at age forty-five and Mulvihill's in Ireland on a vacation," he thought. "Jesus H. Christ!"

Roy, Gene, and Donald honored their older brother's wishes and agreed not to continue the case. It was obviously just going to be too painful for Raymond.

But Gene woke up one morning and immediately called Roy.

"Brother, there's only one thing left to do," he said. "We have to try and close this thing out."

"I know what you're talking about," responded Roy. "It might even help ease Ray's pain. He's been carrying around so much for so many years. Do you think we'll get any cooperation?"

"Probably not. But we have to try."

"Okay, let's go for it."

Later that day, Gene called the Catholic Charities of Kansas City, Missouri, seeking information about Darlene's son. He was immediately transferred to the appropriate caseworker, who just happened to be in the building.

"We want to find him, meet him, and let him know who his mother was and that he has five uncles," Gene told her.

The caseworker asked Gene if there was any documentation he might be able to send her. She did not, however, mention that she had been in contact with Darlene's son or that she was conducting a comprehensive search.

Gene agreed to send her a copy of the first page of Darlene's photo album, her death certificate, and a few other key pieces of information. He also asked her to call his brother, Roy, in California for additional material.

"Thank you, Mr. Albert," responded the caseworker. "I'll conduct a search and get back to you when I'm done. But that will be at least a couple of months."

"Okay," said Gene. "Thanks very much."

Four months later, on October 22, 1998, Gene received a telephone call from the caseworker.

"Mr. Albert, your nephew's name is T. J. Smith. I will provide him your phone number and address and your brother's. That's all the information I can give you at this time. It will be up to Mr. Smith whether or not he wants to contact you. But I think you can expect a call."

The next day, the caseworker called T. J. and provided him with all the basic information he had been seeking.

"Mr. Smith, your birth mother's name was Darlene Francis Albert Groetken," she said. "The time of her death was July 25, 1987. She was living in Wichita, Kansas. She is buried at the Calvary Mausoleum in Wichita. She named you Bill Patrick but, of course, your parents changed that with the formal adoption.

"I'm going to mail you a copy of her social history. This is a document that was created when she checked into St. Anthony's Infant Home when she was pregnant. It includes some information on her background, education and employment, her relatives, a physical description, and so on. It also includes some references to your birth father. Let me read you a few things.

"'This young man is twenty-one years of age and of Irish nationality extraction. He is described as six feet tall and weight is estimated at 160 pounds. He too is dark in coloring and has brown hair and brown eyes. He finished high school, and the last job he had was as a clerk. Alleged father was Catholic and had been baptized in infancy. His general health is excellent and mother knows of no negatives that would deter placement.'

"Mr. Smith, you have five uncles living throughout the United States. The two I have spoken to are Mr. Gene Albert and Mr. Roy Albert. They are anxious to meet you. I hope that contact with your uncles will help answer many of the questions that you have had and complete the goal you had when you set out on this search.

"My follow-up letter to you will also include a copy of the opening page of your birth mother's photo album and her death certificate that your uncle sent me. I'm sorry I don't have more, but as you know, I've just tried everything. I've gone through all the other records and I just cannot find anything else. Part of this file is missing."

Three days later, T. J. received the caseworker's file with all the accompanying information and began flipping through the documents. When he came to the first page of Darlene's photo album, he gasped when he saw the picture of the youthful priest at the top of the page.

"My God," he thought to himself. "That's exactly what I looked like when I was in high school. Exactly!"

Chapter Fifty-Four

Shortly after receiving all the information from the case-worker, T. J. called Gene, and the two had quite an extended conversation.

"Darlene was trying to find you just before she died," Gene told him.

"Oh, really?"

"Yeah, we found a lot of her correspondence with the Catholic Charities looking for information about you. But they wouldn't tell her anything. Said it violated a confidentiality agreement."

"I was never contacted by anyone to inform me that my natural mother was trying to find me," said T. J. "Neither were my parents."

"Well, that was over ten years ago."

"Yeah, but I still would liked to have known."

"Are you married?" asked Gene. "Do you have any children?"

"Yes. I married my high school sweetheart and we have two young children."

"Wow, that's great. That's wonderful."

T. J. then proceeded to tell his uncle that he had grown up in Missouri, graduated from college, and also had obtained an MBA.

"Gee, that's terrific," responded Gene. "Darlene would have been very glad to know all that. She would have been very proud."

"What can you tell me about her early years?" asked T. J. "I'm very interested in the Albert family background."

"Well, that's a pretty involved story. There were nine children to begin with."

"Nine?"

"Yeah, six boys and three girls. Darlene was the youngest girl; third oldest child."

Over the next ten or fifteen minutes, Gene related to his nephew much of the family saga—the marriage of his parents, the Martins versus the Alberts, the death of two of the young children, the removal of the others from the home, being placed in the orphanage in El Dorado, going to Boys Town and the various foster homes.

After Gene finished, T. J. expressed his amazement. "That's an unbelievable story," he said. "And, you know, the only town in the state of Kansas I've ever lived in was El Dorado."

"Really?"

"Yes. I had a summer job there when I was in college."

"Well, that's real close to the orphanage," replied Gene. "Did you ever hear about the St. Joseph Home for Children?"

"No, never did. Tell me, was Darlene living in Wichita at the time?"

"What year was that, again?"

"1983."

"Yeah, sure she was. She was living by herself in an apartment on North Market Street—#203, I think it was. Her husband, Tom Groetken, died just the year before."

"Just curious, but what was his middle name?"

"Joseph," I think.

"T. J.—same initials as me."

"Wow, what a coincidence," said Gene.

[Silence]

"You know," continued T. J., "that summer in 1983, I used to make the forty-five-minute drive into Wichita about once a month with a buddy of mine. It was usually on the weekends and we'd almost always go to the Cowboy Bar on Kellogg. Do you know the place?"

"Yeah, sure," replied Gene. "Used to go there all the time, myself. As a matter of fact, it's only a couple of miles from where Darlene lived."

"Do you think she ever went there?"

"Well, she might have. But if she did, it probably wasn't very often. Darlene pretty much kept to herself in those last few years. We didn't see each other that much."

"Gosh, it boggles my mind to think that you or she might have actually been in the Cowboy Bar at the same time I was there."

"Oh, I know. What an odd twist."

"Gene, tell me something, will you? Who is this priest at the top of the photo album?"

All of a sudden Gene became apprehensive and fidgety.

"Umm . . . well, er, that's Father Daniel Mulvihill."

"Well, what does he have to do with all this?" asked T. J.

"Uhhh . . . ummm, he was a priest who was in El Dorado. He, uh, was a pastor at St. John's Church next to the orphanage when we were there."

"Anything else? I mean why did Darlene have him on the first page of her photo album?"

"Ummm . . . well, he was Irish. I remember that much. He was also the boys basketball coach. I played on the team."

"Okay," said T. J., not wanting to push the subject. "Listen, I need to hang up now. I'd like to call your brother, Roy, in California and talk to him for a little while."

"Okay, T. J. Thanks for calling. Talk to you later."

When T. J. got Roy on the phone, the two exchanged pleasantries and some of the same basic information that he and Gene had discussed. Then T. J. brought up Father Mulvihill.

"What did Gene tell you?" asked Roy.

"Well, not very much. He just seemed real nervous about the whole thing and I didn't want to press him on it."

Roy then just blasted out the whole sordid story—about how the brothers believed that Mulvihill was his real father; about how he had carried on a relationship with Darlene since she was thirteen or fourteen years old; about how he had followed her when she was placed in a foster home in Walnut, Kansas, and became the priest at a parish in Pittsburg; about how he had then moved back to Wichita after she did; about how he had carried on with her; about how he drove her to Kansas City and checked her into St. Anthony's; and about how he had pursued her after she returned.

Stunned, T. J. just sat back in his chair and listened. He'd always had a pretty thick skin, but this was just too astonishing not to have an emotional impact.

After hanging up with Roy, he immediately placed a call to an old friend of the Smith family who also happened to be a Catholic priest. Coincidentally, this was the same priest who had, for a time, been pastor of St. Mark's church in Wichita and had actually become acquainted with Darlene and her husband—although T. J. Smith was unaware of this fact.

The priest had gone to the seminary with the brother of T. J.'s father. And because he didn't have any family of his own, he was kind of adopted by the Smiths. As a matter of fact, the priest had attended all the family gatherings while T. J. was growing up and T. J. usually referred to him as "Uncle."

"I need to ask you a couple of questions," said T. J. as soon as his adopted uncle got on the telephone.

"Sure, T. J. What is it?"

"Did you ever run across a priest named Daniel Mulvihill?"

"Oh sure, we did a hand-off on a parish many years ago."

"What can you tell me about him?"

"Well, I didn't know him all that well. He was part of the Irish community of priests. They were a very unique group of people, very cliquish, very tight, you know. I always got the feeling that I was something of an outsider to them. You know, always treated a little differently because I was not from Ireland."

"Well, tell me, do you know what church he's at now?"

"He's not at a church anymore, T. J. Word I got was that they retired him because of a paternity suit."

Chapter Fifty-Five

In early December 1995, T. J. Smith decided to travel to Wichita to meet his newly found uncles. And Ray, Gene, and Dean happily agreed to meet him for dinner.

As soon as T. J. walked into the lobby, the brothers were struck by his resemblance to Darlene around the eyes. But they all agreed later that he was the spitting image of Daniel Mulvihill—tall and good-looking, he even had the same pleasant smile. Everybody shook hands kind of uneasily and then piled into Ray's van to drive the few miles to the Steak and Sirloin restaurant.

After everybody had ordered, Ray leaned forward and smiled at his nephew. "T. J., did you know that today, December third, was Darlene's birthday? She would have been fifty-seven years old."

"No I didn't know that," he responded. "What a coincidence."

Then T. J. paused for a moment and said: "I've got another coincidence for you."

"What's that?" asked Ray.

"Tomorrow is my adopted mom's birthday."

"No kidding?"

"Yup, no kidding."

The rest of the dinner conversation centered around their immediate families. Ray and Dean talked about their children, Gene about Esther and her mother, and T. J. proudly showed some pictures of his family.

"Mind if I have that picture of you and your family?" asked Ray.

"Not at all, Ray," said T. J. handing it over. "Here, take it."

Just before the check came, Gene reached into his pocket and pulled out a couple of friendship rings.

"T. J., these belonged to Darlene," he said passing the rings across the table. "We wanted you to have them."

"Gee, thanks, fellas. I appreciate this very much. Really."

On the drive back to the hotel, Ray asked T. J. if he might want to stop by and visit Darlene's grave.

"She's buried in the Mausoleum at the Catholic cemetery," he said. "It's right off this road on the way back to the hotel."

"Okay, why don't we do that. But it's getting kind of dark. Will we be able to see anything?"

"Oh, sure," said Gene. "They have a light in there."

A few minutes later, Ray pulled the van into the Calvary cemetery parking lot and the four men got out and walked up the steps to the mausoleum. When they got inside, Dean pointed up to the left at the granite vaults.

"She's right up there," he said.

T. J. gazed upward and saw the inscription: "Darlene Albert Groetken, 1941–1987." Then he looked at some of the other names buried nearby.

"Look at this," he said. "There are three or four bishops. I guess this is a pretty prestigious place for church leaders in the Wichita Catholic diocese, huh?"

"Indeed it is," said Dean.

"Look over here, T. J.," said Gene. "There's the crypt of Bishop Christian D. Winkleman right across from Darlene."

"Why would you single him out over the others?" asked T. J.

"Because he's the bishop who founded the orphan's home in El Dorado."

"Wow!" said T. J. "That's incredible!"

When they arrived back at the hotel, Ray, Gene, and Dean saw their nephew back into the lobby.

"We knew you and Darlene would eventually have found each other if she had lived," Gene said to T. J. "And we're so glad we've been able to meet you."

"You know," said T. J., "I really had a desire to find her. When I found out she had died, my hopes, at first, were dashed because I wanted to personally tell her 'thank you' for everything."

Ray's eyes began to moisten as he listened to T. J. "Why did you want to do that?" he asked softly.

"Because she brought me into the world. I'll be forever grateful to Darlene for giving me life. I've been blessed with a lot of wonderful things. My adoptive parents are wonderful, loving, spiritual people. And the Catholic church was a very positive force in my life. I was able to go to college and start my own business. I have a wonderful family. I'm a lucky guy, Ray. I'm so lucky. And I just wanted to tell her thank you for giving me life."

Before they left to go home, Ray, Gene, and Dean each gave T. J. a long, sustained hug. They hugged him for themselves. And they hugged him, most especially, for their sister Darlene.

She would have wanted them to do it.

She would have liked that.

Chapter Fifty-Six

When Ray got back to his apartment that night, he grabbed a beer out of the refrigerator, picked up Darlene's photo album, and plopped himself down on the couch. As he flipped through the pictures his sister had very carefully and lovingly placed on every page—as he looked through endless photos of nuns and priests intermingled with his parents, grandparents, brothers and sisters, nieces and nephews—it suddenly hit him. This wasn't so much a photo album as it was a *family* album.

The picture of Darlene and Mulvihill on the front page with the child in between was *her* immediate family. They'd had a child together—she and this Catholic priest. She went to Catholic schools, was taught by nuns, and was raised in a Catholic orphanage. *That's* why the 1957 "class photo" at the El Dorado children's home was front and center on the first page. Darlene must have felt that the Catholic church was the only real family she ever had. *That's* why she was buried at the Calvary Mausoleum with all the bishops instead of at St. Mark's with Joe, Clara, Mary Ann, and Lonnie Lee. She must have figured Mulvihill would be buried there, too.

This photo album, then, told Darlene's story. She had never shown it to anyone while she was alive. But she had left it behind. Why? Well, obviously because she wanted people to know. But who? Her brothers? No. She probably put the entire album together for the son she had been searching for.

"I'll bet that's it," Ray said to himself. "I'm going to give this album to T. J., then. That had to be what Darlene had in mind."

Then Ray began to think about his own life.

He thought about how little Lonnie Lee had died and how his mom had asked him if he'd rolled over on him. He'd always thought he might have killed his little brother in his sleep. But with all this research they'd done recently, he had finally seen that the death certificate had listed "malnutrition" as the cause of death. So it hadn't been his fault, after all.

He thought about how he and his brothers and sisters had been taken away from their parents. He had always believed that he should somehow have been able to prevent it. But he was only ten years old back then. He couldn't have prevented it. There was nothing he could have done. And all that time he wanted to get his brothers and sisters out of the orphanage and back together—and get his mother out of Larned—he was powerless to have done anything.

And he was only twelve years old when that thing with Sister Agnesina happened. That wasn't his fault, either. Hell, he was just a kid. The Catholic church said it never happened, that she was never there. But he knew the truth. She was there. It happened the way he said. What did he care if they refused to believe him?

What happened to his sisters, Norma Jean and Darlene, wasn't his fault, either. He couldn't have made any difference. He couldn't have prevented Norma Jean's mental problems or Mulvihill from taking advantage of Darlene. The Catholic church might have been able to prevent it, but not him.

Then Ray began to think that maybe he was wrong to hold the entire Catholic church responsible for everything that happened to him and his family. After all, Darlene's son had said he was a devout Catholic and that the church had been a positive force in his life. And by the grace of God, T. J. turned out great, just great. Maybe most of the Catholic church, then, was good. Maybe what happened to his family was uncommon—an aberration, a rarity. Yes, maybe he could look at it that way from now on.

With that thought, Ray suddenly felt a huge sense of relief. Somehow, knowing the entire story seemed to loosen the shackles of a burden that had been forever weighing him down.

Quickly, he jumped up and pulled his Bible off the book-shelf. Within a few seconds, he found the quote that had suddenly popped into his mind.

Then he lifted the book up to the light and read Isaiah 10:27 aloud, as if to convince himself that, at long last, it might finally be true:

> *And it shall come to pass in that day, that his burden shall be taken away from off thy shoulder, and his yoke from off thy neck, and the yoke shall be destroyed . . .*

Afterword

In mid-twentieth century America, orphanages and infant homes operated by the Catholic church were clearly modeled after those already established in Ireland. The decades-long influx of Irish priests into the United States ensured it.

Recently, hundreds of middle-aged Irish men and women who were confined in industrial schools as children have begun to speak out. And their stories about daily life are remarkably similar to those related by the Albert family.

Many reported a terrible sense of isolation and loneliness. "Other children used to dance around us singing, 'God help the poor orphans, they're not normal,'" said one. "The worst thing," related another, "was looking through the windows to the street . . . knowing there was nobody to come for you."

Others reported the practice of silence at meals and the perpetual cleaning, scrubbing, and polishing. "I had to scrub sixteen flights of stairs and three corridors," remembered one Irish woman. "If I didn't do it properly, I had to do it all over again."

The most common of the memories, by far, were the enduring feelings that each orphanage was "a place of fear" or a "reign of terror." There were cruel punishments for bed-wetting, whippings for talking or laughing during mass, and children were often awakened in the middle of the night and either beaten, chastised, or forced to perform some sort of chore. "The worst thing that ever happened to me in my life," recalled one man, "was the caning I got when I was eight or nine. The nuns took me out of bed at 12:30 at night. All I could see was the strap flashing past me. I was black and blue all over. I still wake up with awful nightmares of that strap and everything flashing red in front of my eyes."

There were constant beatings for "just looking grubby." Little heads were banged against walls by nuns until "I thought they'd fractured my skull." And children were "locked up in small, dark rooms" sometimes "for days with nothing to eat." There was also confusing behavior by the nuns, some of whom "made us undress in front of them and then they beat us," and others who would lecture the children that "your bodies are the Temple of the Holy Ghost—they are sacred, and should not be touched."

Less reported, but still pervasive, were many stories of sexual abuse and pedophilia. These acts were reported to be perpetrated mostly by priests and/or "brothers" rather than by nuns. But fewer reports of child sexual abuse may be due to the victims' unwillingness to discuss what happened.

Medical and psychiatric publications have extensively documented how sexually abused children may be impacted for the rest of their lives. CSA (child sexual abuse) survivors are often hostage to their own thought processes, implanted by their abusers, and from which they may never be totally released. Some endure with their "fingers in the dike" until they explode like "a ticking time bomb." Others display extreme and unpredictable changes in behavior, that include rage, hostility, and anger. They suffer from self-blame, relationship difficulties, denial, and dissociation. Often, they experience problems with drug and alcohol abuse and promiscuity. And many develop mental illnesses such as depression, paranoia, and multiple personality disorders.

After being released from the industrial schools, many Irish girls took jobs cleaning houses, offices, and other buildings because "that's all we knew how to do." Several reported moving "from one domestic job to another." One said she worked "as a domestic in the Bishop's home."

Numerous young women became promiscuous or drifted into prostitution. One Catholic lay organization completed a report on local prostitution that noted: "the greater proportion of those involved are illegitimate orphans who have spent the greater portion of their childhood in orphanages and convents." Quite a few of the girls who have spoken out had illegitimate children of their own. Others married and raised large broods. But the husbands they chose often drank too much and were physically abusive.

Many of the young men who had been in the orphanages reported later having serious problems with drugs and alcohol. As adults, they moved from place to place, never feeling they were home or that they belonged. Often they lived alone and never married. Those who did refused to have children and experienced higher-than-average rates of divorce. Moreover, one government study determined that at least half of the homeless men in Ireland had spent their childhoods in industrial schools. Sixty percent of those were listed as "social and vocational failures" while twenty percent were categorized as "borderline" (in and out of jobs).

Both men and women reported experiencing repressed memories and an inability to cope with "endless nightmares." Some said they had been "in and out of mental hospitals for years." One woman remarked that she had "tried to kill myself three times—always when I'd been drinking. I couldn't see the point in living any more."

Some Irish psychiatrists have reported that many children who endured the industrial schools and maternity homes (or laundries) were scarred for life, both physically and mentally. And once they discovered that a patient had spent his or her childhood in an orphanage, there was very little that could be done because the usual emotional development had just not taken place. They also noted that young women who had experienced time in the laundries and had given up their illegitimate babies for adoption, usually pushed the pain way down and, as a result, lived "tortured lives" often marked by prostitution, abusive relationships, divorce, alcohol abuse, and mental illness. Furthermore, thirty years after the fact, birth mothers and adopted children both experienced irrepressible desires to find each other. And they'd go to great lengths to do so, despite often being met by uncooperative church officials.

And one overwhelming commonality among Irish men and women who survived the various Catholic-operated institutions was the fact that they wanted nothing more to do with the church.

"Are you joking?" said one woman when asked if she practiced her religion. "I've never been to church since," said another. "I've spent all my life escaping from the orphanage."

The orphanage that housed the seven Albert children, the St. Joseph Home for Children-Lewis E. Allen Memorial in El Dorado, Kansas, finally ceased operations on December 23, 1959. At the time, there were only five children in residence. After years of being on a "standby," temporary usage status, the Wichita diocese converted it into a nursing home for the aged operated by the Little Sisters of the Poor, part of the St. Joseph order of nuns. The building was remodeled in 1978 and then served as a family life center where Catholic youth meetings and marriage and engagement encounters were held. In the mid-1990s, it was sold into private ownership. Currently, it is an apartment complex abounding with young children who roam the halls and grounds. During its seventeen years of operation, the St. Joseph Home housed 540 children. It was the only Catholic orphanage in the history of the state of Kansas.

St. Anthony's Infant Home in Kansas City, Missouri, where Darlene Albert and hundreds of other young, unmarried women went to spend their pregnancies, changed its name to the St. Anthony Home in 1964. At that time, a change in policy sent the newborn babies directly from St. Mary's Hospital to foster homes until they could be placed out for adoption. It ceased operations as a maternity home on September 15, 1969 when it was converted into a Catholic family and community services center. In 1986, the Catholic Archdiocese of Kansas City sold the building to Welcome House, an alcoholic rehabilitation agency.

In addition to the lawsuits brought by the Albert brothers and *Gravley v. Blanpied,* the Catholic Diocese of Wichita was, at the same time, confronted with charges of child sexual abuse by another priest. Father Robert K. Larsen was accused by a number of parents of molesting their young sons while they served as altar boys in his care. At first, the diocese transferred Larsen to another parish (in Newton, Kansas) but, when locals found out about the charges, Larsen was forced to retire. He subsequently moved out of state. Reverend Ronald M. Gilmore, the vicar general who wrote the April 20, 1995, letter to Roy Albert denying the brothers' accusations, handled all these complaints. He was promoted in 1996 and today serves as Bishop of the Catholic Diocese of Dodge City, Kansas.

Father William A. Wheeler died at the age of eighty-three on October 3, 1994—2 months after Roy Albert first told the Albert brothers' story to Rev. Gilmore.

Little Patty (name changed by request), the nine-year-old who was singled out by Father Wheeler to accompany him on rounds to Eureka, August, and Byrne, Kansas, is a divorced mother of three living in the southwestern United States. Hundreds of other "Home" children are scattered around Kansas and the rest of the country. Joe Kaiser received subsistence checks from the Catholic church for years after leaving the orphanage. He died of brain cancer in 1978 at the age of twenty-nine.

Sister Agnesina Metzinger died on June 18, 1978 at the age of sixty-four.

Father Daniel B. Mulvihill retired on May 19, 1996, three days after the Albert brothers filed their lawsuit. He had triple heart bypass surgery in 1999 and today lives in a Catholic retirement community in Wichita.

Marlys Marshall, the Alberts' attorney, married a former priest in the Wichita diocese. She lives in the southwestern United States.

T. J. Smith [name changed by request] owns his own business. He and his family live in the southeastern United States.

Norma Jean Albert spent the last twelve years of her life in and out of halfway houses, detox centers, and mental wards in Wichita. She married for a third time to the son of a woman who owned a halfway house she was staying in at the time. On the afternoon of September 27, 1991, neighbors found her on her hands and knees in her backyard "drinking a fifth of whiskey and eating dirt and grass." Hallucinating badly, she was taken by ambulance to the mental ward of a detox center at 610 North Broadway. After being administered a drug designed to quell her hallucinations, she passed out. An employee found her dead in bed the next morning. Norma Jean Albert was fifty-one years old.

After graduating from Boys Town in 1961, Dean Albert worked in the data processing department for Cudahy Packing Company, served in the US Army, and held various jobs with Bell Telephone, Federal Reserve Bank, Liberty Loan, and JI Case. He was married for eighteen years and had seven children—all of whom have graduated from college. In 1988, after his marriage fell apart, he became suicidal and was treated for severe depression. He temporarily moved in with his twin brother, Gene, and Gene's wife, Esther. For the next seven years, Dean held various odd jobs that included making deliveries for pharmacies and mowing lawns. He has worked for the Wichita Water Department since 1996.

Donald Albert returned to Wichita in 1963. Over the next three years, he worked for Cudahy Packing Company, Cessna Aircraft, and Boeing. From 1972 to 1977 he worked for the United States Postal Service. Then he abruptly quit and went out to California to live for a couple of years with his brother, Roy. There he bounced from odd job to odd job. In 1996, he attended barber's school in Kansas City and was a barber for six months. Next he took a job as a service representative for Ferrymore Seat Company based in Fulton, Kentucky. He was on the road nearly all the time, except in the winter months when he lived in Wichita. For the last few years of his life, he drove a truck based out of Knoxville, Tennessee. He told friends that if he and his brothers would have stayed in the orphanage for a longer period of time, they would have wound up in jail or been shot. "Boys Town saved us all," he said. Donald Albert died on February 16, 2001 from lymphoma. He never married.

Gene Albert graduated from Boys Town in 1962 and worked at Henry's Clothing Store for four years as a fitter of men's clothing—then as a sheet metal worker at Cessna Aircraft for one year. In July of 1968, he joined the US Postal Service in Wichita and still works there today. In 1996, Gene took Rev. Gilmore up on his offer to undergo a psychological evaluation. He spent an hour and a half answering several hundred questions on paper and then was interviewed by a psychologist for fifteen minutes. Afterwards, Gene was informed he suffered from "approach avoidance" syndrome. He and Esther have no children.

Roy Albert got out of Boys Town in 1966 and worked in Wichita for six months before joining the Army. After a two-year hitch, he spent one year in college at Wichita State. Then he moved to Denver for a year and worked at Miller Tire Company before heading back to Wichita and picking up a job at a local funeral home. He moved to San Francisco in 1973 and, for the next twenty years, was employed at the US Postal Service and the Santa Fe Railroad. For the past decade, he has done consulting work. He has never married. Since his memories of child sexual abuse returned, Roy has been a regular attendee at local meetings of SNAP (Survivors Network of Those Abused by Priests), a national organization with roots in Chicago. On March 25, 2000, he attended an emotional "Apology Liturgy for Clergy Abuse Victims" held by the Catholic Diocese of Oakland. "The failure of many of the leaders of the Catholic church to confront this abuse head-on, to . . . remove priest abusers and other employees from active ministry, or to take the side of the victims, has been one of the more distressing aspects of the church's recent history," said Bishop John S. Cummins. About 130 fellow clergy, victims, and their families attended the service. In a television interview afterwards, Roy Albert was asked how he felt. "Well, it didn't come from the Wichita diocese where my abuse occurred," he said. "And I still look at most priests as pedophiles. But it's a beginning."

Ray Albert lives in a small apartment by himself in Wichita and still travels around Kansas four to five days a week stocking and setting up convenience stores. He spends as much time as possible with his brothers, children, grandchildren, and his nieces and nephews. A couple of years ago, he had an operation on his right ear (the one twisted by Sister Flora when he was twelve years old)—and now has 50 percent of its hearing restored. He does not interact with the Catholic church. "I still believe in God, I still pray, and I believe in life hereafter," he has said. "But I don't believe in the church."

Also by Donald T. Phillips

Lincoln on Leadership

On the Brink (with Norman Brinker)

Lincoln Stories for Leaders

The Founding Fathers on Leadership

A Diamond in Spring

Martin Luther King, Jr. on Leadership

Leading with the Heart (with Mike Krzyzewski)

Run to Win

Five-Point Play (with Mike Krzyzewski)

Character in Action (with Adm. James M. Loy, Ret.) [Summer 2003]

Index

St. Joseph Home for
Children-Lewis E. Allen
Memorial
Alberts go to Boys Town,
87–91
Alberts arrive, 28–30, 44–46
daily routine for children,
47–51
in Darlene's keepsakes, 4
founding of, 50–51
last years of, 76–78, 88
physical abuse at, 54–55, 67,
78, 88
present-day status, 222
sexual abuse at, 57–60, 78,
85–86, 88–91
St. Mark's Catholic Church,
166, 169
St. Patrick's Guild, 36
St. Patrick's Institute, 41
St. Vincent de Paul, 34
State Reformatory for Boys,
100

T
Tolbert, B. E. "Jack," 198–200
Tolbert, Pearl, 198–200

V
Viola, Sister, 48

W
Walter, Charles, 80, 81
Wesley Medical Center, 155,
157
Wheeler, Fr. William A., 10–11,
76–78, 82–91, 100–102,
183, 186, 223
Wheeler, Janet F., 5, 8, 102,
145, 172. *See also* Albert,
Darlene Francis
Wichita Children's Home, 21,
22, 25
Winkleman, Bishop Christian
D., 50

Y
York, Fr. Edward, 160

Z
Zimmerman, Carol. *See* Albert,
Carol Zimmerman